Listening to Spoken English

SECOND EDITION

GILLIAN BROWN

LONGMAN
LONDON AND NEW YORK

Longman Group UK Limited,
Longman House, Burnt Mill, Harlow,
Essex CM20 2JE, England
and Associated Companies throughout the world.

Published in the United States of America by Longman Inc., New York

First edition © Longman Group Limited 1977
Second edition © Longman Group UK Ltd

First edition published 1977
Second edition published 1990
Second impression 1991

British Library Cataloguing in Publication Data
Brown, Gillian, *1937–*
    Listening to spoken English. – 2nd ed – (Applied linguistics
    and language study).
    1. English spoken language
    I. Title   II. Series
    428.3

ISBN 0-582-05297-1

Library of Congress Cataloging-in-Publication Data
Brown, Gillian.
        Listening to spoken English/Gillian Brown.—2nd ed.
        p. cm.—(Applied linguistics and language study)
        Includes bibliographical references.
        ISBN 0-582-05297-1
        1. English language—Spoken English.   I. Title.   II. Series.
PE1135.B693   1990   89-13373
421'.5—dc20   CIP

Printed in Malaysia
by Peter Chong Printers Sdn. Bhd.,
Ipoh, Perak Darul Ridzuan

Contents

General editor's preface

Introducing a second edition of what has been a remarkably successful contribution to the *Applied Linguistics and Language Study* Series is
one of the better ways of beginning a new decade in Applied Linguistics, especially when, as with Gillian Brown's book, we are able
to look back with confidence at the impact of the original edition on
the state of the art.

At that time, it was possible to regard Listening as a poor sister
of work in Applied Linguistics, and for several reasons. The over-
whelming concern of most available Language Teaching courses with
the development of oral fluency had led many to assume that the
teaching of the spoken language (what Gillian Brown calls 'slow
colloquial') naturally developed the learner's *listening* competence, in
short, that listening skill would follow the development of spoken
competence. Secondly, research into the processes of second language reading was much further advanced at that time than com-
parable work in Listening; indeed, a glance at the research literature
indicates that it is only relatively recently that Listening has begun
to feature strongly in published work in Applied Linguistics. Thirdly,
a pedagogic preference for making connections between phonetic
ability and speaking rather than with listening cut Listening off from
what now seems an equally natural link to the receiver as well as the
utterer of spoken messages. One might add here, too, that the then
prevailing view of conversation as a speaker to hearer process, rather
than as a mutually informing interaction again marginalised Listening
in favour of spoken competence. To this we must also add, the lack
of empirical research at that time into learners' listening strategies,
the processes of Listening, if you like, and a corresponding uncertainty as to how one might go about designing appropriately motivated
listening syllabuses to parallel the familiar contours of those target-
ting speaking.

In short, Gillian Brown's first edition was a pioneering work. She
showed that the implied natural development of listening competence
from speaking competence was not warranted, partly because of the

lack of identity between the slow formal delivery of the pronunciation drill and the wide range of pronunciation styles encountered by the foreign listener to native speakers, and partly because the emphasis on mastery of the phonological code (whether segmental sounds or tonal contours) had been at the expense of relating auditory signals to the message structure of the discourse. Of course, as language teaching over the last decade became more influenced by work in pragmatics and discourse analysis, this latter discrepancy became only more acute, and her argument in consequence the more telling.

Assessment of the performance of non-native English speaking students in the context of listening to lectures has only served to highlight the need for practice in comprehending messages amid the simplifications of informal speech. A training in listening only to **how** something is being said has been shown to militate against the ability in such a mode to perceive, interpret and retain **what** is being said. In her Chapter 4 on **Patterns of Simplification in Informal Speech** Gillian Brown examines in some detail assimilations and elisions in connected spoken text, with a wide range of illustrative examples, stressing the need for students to discover similar examples in the text they are exposed to and to reflect on the amendments to the phonotactics of 'slow colloquial' English speech instanced in informal styles of speaking.

Notwithstanding the social psychological and pragmatic problems attending the correlation of speech style with interpersonal evaluation and attitude, the *Journal of Language and Social Psychology* regularly attests to the pervasive linkages that are routinely made, often in quite critical social contexts and often with adverse social consequences for the discriminated participants. Gillian Brown's Chapter 6 on **Para-linguistic Features** continues in consequence to be very timely, especially in its rewritten and extended form in this edition. She shows very clearly how attitude can be associated with a range of vocal features (pitch, volume, tempo, placing in voice range), thus indicating to the teacher the parameters within which attitude itself can be described phonetically (*he spoke/exclaimed sadly/warmly/sexily*), but also suggesting how these features can be used as signposts to guide the listener through the structure of spoken argument.

In her final, totally recast Chapter on **Teaching Listening Comprehension**, Gillian Brown not only lays out the framework for a listening syllabus but incidentally offers from a practical perspective what a theory of listening needs to account for. Here she brings together current research into 'top-down' and 'bottom-up' language processing, the issue of variable interpretation of the same acoustic signals, the links to be made between stress allocation and information salience and the connections to be recognised between the vocal and the kinesic in human communication. The breadth of the applied linguistic model offered in this Chapter is of much wider significance than the ostensible focus of her book, precisely because it addresses not only the language teaching audience, but also those applied linguists concerned with professional-client communication and with the treatment of the hearing and speech impaired. Moreover, her emphasis on the social context of listening adds strength to the arguments of those whose view of linguistics requires the intersection of the formal and the functional, and she thus provides through her focus on listening a model for applied linguistic research in general.

It will readily be seen, therefore, that this second edition does much more than merely providing an update on the basis of recent research. We can now see how central the study of Listening is to applied linguistics, not only for those concerned with language teaching but more generally, and, moreover, how important its study is for our understanding of the workings of language as a whole. For this widening of our focus we are all deeply in Gillian Brown's debt.

Christopher N Candlin
General Editor,
Macquarie University, Sydney

Acknowledgements

I have to thank many friends and colleagues who have read parts of this manuscript in its first edition and made valuable comments, especially Pit Corder, Julian Dakin, John Laver, John Lyons, Henry Widdowson and my husband, Keith Brown. I am grateful too, to the BBC for permission to quote from broadcast material, and to the many people who have allowed me to record their lectures, seminars, interviews and conversations. I should also particularly like to thank Gordon Walsh of Longman for his meticulous scrutiny of the text and for his wise advice.

Introduction to the second edition

This second edition, prepared nearly fifteen years after the book was originally written, has given me the opportunity to incorporate a great deal of what we now know about the processes of listening comprehension which we did not know then. Occasionally, too, particularly in the chapters on rhythm and on intonation, scholarly work in the intervening years has yielded better descriptions, and there too I have incorporated some of the insights deriving from such work.

For those who are familiar with the first edition, it will be convenient to have some indication of where the main changes lie. Chapter 1 has been largely rewritten to give an outline of current approaches to a model of comprehension of spoken language. Chapter 2 has a new initial section but otherwise remains as it was. Chapter 3 incorporates a new section on 'pause' and how this interacts with rhythm, and rather more on the function of stress. Chapter 4 has an extended initial section but otherwise remains largely as it was. Chapter 5 on intonation contains several sections which have been rewritten to varying extents. Chapter 6 of the first edition has disappeared: in 1977, very little work had been published on 'fillers' and it seemed worth while incorporating a chapter that sat rather oddly with the phonetic/phonological interests of the rest of the book. Now that there is a great industry of descriptions of the forms and functions of these and similar phenomena there seems no reason to retain this early but admittedly primitive account. The chapter on 'Paralinguistic features', now Chapter 6, has some modest rewriting in the early part but considerable rewriting in the last sections. The final chapter on 'Teaching listening comprehension' has grown greatly in length. It still incorporates some material from the original chapter but most of it is completely rewritten.

I should make a stylistic point. I remember holding the opinion when I wrote this book originally that the masculine third person pronoun was properly to be interpreted as neutral as between male and female where no question of different gender was involved. I find, somewhat to my surprise, that my feelings (note that I do not say 'my thoughts') have changed radically. I now find the insistence on the masculine pronoun dated and repetitive. You will be able to recognize those parts of the book which have been rewritten, by the elaborate lengths I go to to avoid using the singular pronoun. Among the original sections that remain there are some expressions of opinion which I now find tendentious but no doubt the present edition will similarly offer its own hostages to the years to come.

Transcription conventions

Symbols in the phonemic transcription are used with the following values:

/ɪ/	as in	pit	/ɪə/	as in	beer
/e/		pet	/eə/		bear
/æ/		pat	/ɑ/		bar/balm
/ɒ/		pot	/ɔ/		court/caught
/ʊ/		put	/ʊə/		tour
/ʌ/		putt	/ɜ/		bird
/ə/		apart	/tʃ/		church
/i/		peat	/dʒ/		judge
/eɪ/		tape	/ŋ/		sing
/aɪ/		type	/θ/		think
/ɔɪ/		boy	/ð/		they
/ju/		tube	/ʃ/		ship
/aʊ/		how	/ʒ/		measure
/əʊ/		hoe	/j/		you
/u/		who			

The vowel symbols used here are those used in *Dictionary of Contemporary English* and in the *English Pronouncing Dictionary* (see Bibliography). However, the length mark /ː/ is not used in this book.

1 The need to teach the comprehension of spoken English

1.1 'Slow colloquial English' and normal speech

There has been a revolution in the teaching of English in the last twenty years. In the early seventies it was still the case that spoken language was the poor relation of written language. Today the importance of teaching the spoken language is universally acknowledged. Much of the energy and imaginativeness of many publishing enterprises is now poured into spoken language materials and it is taken for granted that anyone learning a foreign language needs to be able to use it for talking even though their primary need for it may still be to read or write it. This revolution has ensured that the problems of understanding the spoken form of the foreign language have received increasing attention both in research and in teaching. We now have a much better understanding of the processes of comprehension and there are now many courses on offer which claim to teach listening comprehension, and there are many books and conferences which claim to teach teachers how to improve their students' performance in listening comprehension.

As is often the case in education the pendulum seems to have swung with such violence away from the preoccupations of English language teaching in the period 1950–1979, that some of the concerns and expertise of that period have become, temporarily at least, largely lost. Whereas all trained teachers of English at that time would have received a thorough grounding in the phonetics of English, to prepare them for the job of teaching pronunciation, it is often the case nowadays that teachers emerge from ELT training with little, if any, knowledge of phonetics. This is because the teaching of pronunciation is no longer such a fashionable enterprise as it used to be in many parts of the world. The loss of training in phonetics impinges not only on the teaching of pronunciation but also on the teaching of listening comprehension: one of the problems of listening to a foreign language, though, as I shall make clear, by no means the only one, is that you are listening to the sounds of a foreign language and that they are not organized in the same way as the sounds of your own familiar language. It is harder to determine which bits of the acoustic blur that hit your ears are the beginnings and ends of words, in fact, which bits *are* words, and what words they might be, and harder to determine how they are organized—which bits hang together—and what the speaker might mean by saying them. One of the ways a teacher can help his or her students in understanding a foreign language is to help them find their way around the sounds of the foreign language, to identify the bits which will give them most information, to help them recognize the most important cues to meaning. This involves paying attention to the way English is typically spoken by native speakers, and that is what this book is intended to help you do.

One reason why it is hard to understand a foreign language is that we typically learn the foreign language, particularly if the learning setting is a classroom, in terms of words and sentences. We see words with clear edges written on the board or in books and we learn to write words with spaces between them. The words are organized into sentences which are also clearly demarcated: they might begin with capital letters and end with full stops. When the teacher pronounces these words he or she will tend to pronounce them fairly slowly and clearly, giving us plenty of opportunity to recognize them. Indeed many teachers of foreign languages develop particularly slow, clear styles of speech when speaking the foreign language to learners. In real life, however, ordinary speakers of the foreign language are simply using it to get on with living. They speak only clearly enough to make themselves understood in a particular context. Most of them will speak more slowly and clearly to the deaf and elderly, to young children and to foreigners, especially at the beginning of the conversation when they are particularly aware that the other person needs to be treated with consideration, but many speakers quite quickly adopt a more normal, more rapid style of speech.

Now it may be objected that this is a 'degenerate' and 'slovenly' form of English and that no foreigner ought to be expected to understand it. I have heard this opinion expressed. The answer to this objection is that the situation exists. The native English speaker is not going to reform his speech habits overnight—if an overseas student wishes to understand spoken English, he will have to learn to cope with the English he hears around him. Another difficulty is that many teachers, especially native English teachers, have a very idealistic impression of how English is spoken. Most literate people find it very difficult to disassociate knowledge of how a word is spelt from how it is pronounced. Although such a person may be quite aware that the spoken forms of the words *pale* and *pail* are identical, there nonetheless persists an aura of difference because of the different spelling. Each word retains its own identity—a complex audio-visual identity—even when it is very indistinctly pronounced. And since each meaningful message must be composed of words, it is very hard to suppose that one has somehow heard *less* than a word. Consider for example an agitated mother rounding up her family for a family outing. When at last she has them all assembled she might say: *Ready at last! 's go then.* If one of her family is asked to repeat what she has just said he will repeat it in terms of the words he has understood: *Ready at last. Let's go then.* He will have to have interpreted this little piece of acoustic information which I have symbolized by *'s* as a word, because messages are composed of words, not odd acoustic bits and pieces. Clearly most of the time anyone is listening to English being spoken, he is listening for the meaning of the message—not to how the message is being pronounced. Indeed if you listen to how the words are spoken it is very unlikely that you can simultaneously understand what it is that is being said. On the whole people do not listen critically to the way the message is pronounced. The odd glottal stop or unusual pronunciation of a word may strike the listener, but most of the time he is busy abstracting the meaning of the message, and preparing his own mental comments on it. This is why most people are quite unaware of how English is actually spoken. If asked to listen carefully and critically, with all their phonetic sophistication, to a tape-recording of a speaker, they are usually astonished, and often shocked, to notice how the speaker is speaking. This is even true of sophisticated phonetics students being asked to listen critically to a tape-recording of a perfectly normal and representative radio newsreader. Until one listens to how the message is being spoken, rather than to what is being said, it is perfectly reasonable to have a very idealistic and starry-eyed view of how English is pronounced by public speakers.

This idealistic view is naturally attractive to teachers in that they want to teach 'good' English to their students. Since their main interest is in teaching their students correct pronunciation, they naturally want to find a slow, clear model for the students to imitate. Slow colloquial is an ideal model for their purpose for the following reasons. Each sentence is uttered as a sequence of readily identifiable words. It is repeatable because each word has a very stable phonetic form in this style of English. The teacher can provide a clear model and can hear whether or not the student is copying the model correctly. It is an eminently *teachable* model. It is also valuable in that it ensures that the student copying it will speak slowly and carefully. Even if the foreign student's speech is marred by syntactic and vocabulary flaws, native speakers of English will find this slow careful type of speech reasonably easy to understand. I should like to make it quite clear that I am not suggesting that there is any more suitable model than this for teaching the production of spoken English. On the contrary, I believe slow colloquial to be the only practicable model, at least for all but the most sophisticated students. Very advanced students can of course progress to a model based on English as normally spoken by native speakers. Having said that this is a good model for teaching pronunciation, we should be quite clear that this does not mean it is the only 'correct' or 'acceptable' style of spoken English. It is clear that in a normal English context the notion of 'correctness' needs to be replaced by a notion of 'appropriateness'. If native speakers of English can communicate perfectly efficiently in informal English which is far removed from slow colloquial there is no reasonable sense in which such English may be described as 'incorrect'. There is also nothing to be gained by describing it in such emotionally charged words as 'slipshod' and 'careless'. If this style of pronunciation provides an efficient mode of communication and, at the same time, by the fact that all the members of a group are using the same style of speech, reaffirms their sense of being members of a group, we have to recognize this style as being as appropriate and efficient as any other. Words like 'slovenly' appear to be used as terms of social evaluation prompted by strongly held norms of behaviour rather than as objective descriptive terms.

Pronunciation might reasonably be described as 'careless', 'slipshod' etc. when it functions inefficiently as a mode of communication, when the speaker finds that people just do not understand what he says. The most likely place to find these derogatory terms being used is, of course, the classroom—and the classroom in native English speaking countries just as much as others. The teacher will often tell a child to 'speak up' or to talk more clearly, even if he has understood what the child has said. The reason here seems to partly be that the teacher values highly the child who looks him in the eye and answers clearly, as though he is not ashamed of what he is saying (which seems to be, to some extent at least, a moral and social evaluation), and partly that the teacher is encouraging the child to speak appropriately in a given situation. In the public situation of the classroom, where the child is speaking, as it were, before an audience, it is appropriate for him to speak more clearly than he would in private conversation with one of his friends. The notion of the appropriateness of speaking loudly enough in public so that everyone can hear you, is presumably part of the same cultural code which insists that it is rude to whisper in front of other people—no member of the group must feel himself to be excluded because he cannot hear what is being said. Whereas, in the native English situation, the teacher can rely on the child learning to speak and listen appropriately in the everyday situations that arise outside the classroom, in countries where English is not the first language there is a danger that students may never develop the ability to use an appropriate style of pronunciation in such situations. This in itself may not be too unfortunate since the foreign speaker will probably sound foreign to some extent anyway—though it always seems a shame when one meets foreign speakers of English with a very impressive command of spoken English who speak in conversation as though they were addressing a public meeting. What is very unfortunate and much more important is that such students are not given any opportunity to learn to understand an informal style of speech.

I have been talking so far as if there were only two styles of speech in English—slow colloquial and the informal, almost conversational speech used by many public speakers. This is of course a vast oversimplification. There are certainly more than two styles of speech, indeed there are an infinite number and they have no definable boundaries, each merges imperceptibly into the next. We can construct a scale which will show us the impossibility of stating a definite number of styles. At the most informal end of the scale let us put two people who know each other very well and are familiar with each other's speech, way of life, mode of thought—husband and wife for example, intimate friends, long-standing colleagues. Such people will often exchange a remark that even a third native speaker of the same accent and general background cannot understand. The next point along the scale may be represented by our first couple and this third person—they will have to be slightly more explicit in a conversation with him. We can then add other people to this group who may speak with a different accent, be members of a different social group, come from a different background. With each of these variables the utterances must become more explicit—and if one of the members of the group differs from the others in all these variables the others will have to make a considerable effort to make clear what they are saying. So even in the context of small group discussion we can expect several different styles of speech. If we were now to begin to vary the context—to place our speakers in public meetings, private formal meetings, and so on, and to vary the members of the group so that it might include one very distinguished individual, much admired, perhaps even feared by the other members of the group, we shall see that other styles, no single one uniquely identifiable, will emerge. A foreign student in Britain or in any other country where English is the main native language may find himself in any or all of these situations but the one I am concerned with here is when he finds himself as a member of a group of native speakers of English, being taught by a native speaker of English, and participating in discussions with the group. I shall call the style of English found in this situation 'informal'. And I shall include within 'informal' the style of speech used in radio and television broadcast discussions. 'Informal' will obviously have many shades within it, but in general I shall describe it as though it were a homogeneous style and compare it explicitly with a 'formal', 'slow colloquial' style of speech.

Students whose education has been largely couched in slowly and deliberately spoken English are often shocked to find, when they enter a context in which native speakers are talking to each other, that they have considerable difficulty in understanding what is being said. The foreign student may have a good command of spoken English—may speak fluently and comprehensibly and be able to understand speech which is deliberately addressed to a foreign student or intended to be listened to by foreigners, but such students enter a quite different realm when they try to follow speech which is primarily addressed to native speakers. This is a common experience for visitors to Britain, and for students who come to follow courses in colleges and universities. The phenomenon will also be experienced as students leave the relatively carefully articulated programmes of the BBC World Service and tune to radio and television programmes intended for a native-speaking audience. Even BBC newsreaders, whose speech was once subject to careful analysis by phoneticians who were employed to cultivate the 'best possible' pronunciation among this elite corps of broadcasters, have now descended from those Olympian heights and they read the news for the most part in a casual, relatively informal style, just like a member of the public might. There are relics of a former era which can be observed when the death of a famous individual, or some appalling accident which has caused many deaths is announced: in these circumstances news broadcasters regularly lower the pitch of their voices, and speak more slowly and clearly. In general, however, they speak as naturally as if they were talking to someone they know, rather than to a huge, anonymous audience which might include listeners for whom English is not the first language. Similarly, the style of public speaking in the late twentieth century, of actors on stage as well as in the cinema, of teachers and university lecturers is an informal, almost conversational, style where the speaker wishes each member of the audience to react as though he or she were being personally addressed by the speaker who is a friendly and approachable human being.

You will observe that I am talking about a 'public' manner of speech rather than private intimate speech. This is because I believe that it is the public manner of speech which has most dramatically changed in the last forty years or so. This book will be largely concerned with talking about this 'public' style of speech, rather than trying to give a description of the much more attenuated style of speech which may be encountered in informal conversations between people who know each other very well. It is already often a cause of astonishment and, often, disapproval for people who are not used to paying attention to the phonetic detail of speech to analyse carefully speech which is produced in the 'public' manner. As will be seen in Chapter 4 of this book, we have to strain the conventions of phonetic representation in order to draw attention to features of this type of speech—speech, for instance, heard on BBC news. It is frequently not possible to come up with a satisfactory phonetic representation of speech even in this mode. When we come to listen to recordings of relaxed conversations between people who know each other well, 'private' speech, the stretches of obscure acoustic blur often no longer permit any representation on a segment-by-segment basis. A much more sophisticated representation which involves noting how the various articulators which contribute to speech are moving over syllable-sized or even larger stretches of speech is necessary here.

There is a further reason for concentrating on the 'public' style of speech—this is the style of speech which is typically used to transmit information. We can identify two major functions of language: one is 'transactional' and is concerned with transmitting information; the other is 'interactional' and is concerned with the establishment and maintenance of human relationships. Naturally both functions often occur together, since even if your primary concern is to give somebody information, you will always try to present that information in a way that will make it comprehensible, and, usually, acceptable, to the person you are speaking to. However, we can identify instances of language use where the *focus* of the speaker's attention is on the transmission of information and this is particularly clear in examples of 'public' speech: speeches, broadcasts, debates, announcements at railway stations, lectures, and educational classes of all kinds. This is not necessarily the most important function for a student of English to master, but for many students it is a very important function, since their main reason for learning English may be to study in English. The discussion in this book will in general lean on examples of 'public' English which is spoken to be understood by many listeners, and where the function of the language is primarily to give information to the listener. This seems a reasonable minimal level for students who wish to pursue advanced courses in English to try to attain.

1.2 'Testing' or 'teaching' comprehension?

For many years it was suggested that students would learn to understand the spoken form of the language simply by being exposed to it. Many courses which purport to 'teach' listening comprehension in fact consist of exercises which expose the students to a chunk of spoken material on a tape and then ask 'comprehension questions' to try to find out whether or not the student has understood the language of the text. This does not seem so much an example of 'teaching' as of 'testing'. The students are not receiving any help in learning how to process this unfamiliar language—they are simply being given the opportunity of finding out for themselves how to cope. Many of them, of course, will not learn how to do this satisfactorily and they will undergo repeated experience of failure and, as a consequence, may choose to withdraw from learning this unfamiliar language. The great contribution that the teacher can make is to give the student the experience of success.

In order to do this, the teacher needs as good an understanding as we currently have of the nature of comprehension and the processes of comprehension. I shall briefly address these two points.

1.2.1 The nature of comprehension

The traditional model of comprehension supposes that there is an idea in a speaker's head; he or she encodes this into words; the listener hears the speaker's words; he or she 'understands' them, which means that the listener now has the idea which the speaker originally had. Understanding in this model presupposes an exchange of ideas, mediated by language. It is a model which is particularly attractive still to people who work with computers and are impressed by the computational model of language.

It is not difficult to demonstrate, however, that this is not a good account of how human beings understand language. I once gave a 20 minute lecture to a group of six mature, experienced teachers of English. I had prepared copious notes on my lecture and I asked them to take detailed notes of what I said. At the end of this we compared notes—you will not be surprised to learn that there were some remarkable differences between them. Different individuals paid attention to different points which meshed with their own previous experience and interests in different ways. The crucial thing to remember is that human beings each have a unique experience of life behind them, a unique cast of mind, a unique set of interests. At a trivial level such a set of listeners would doubtless agree on what was said in a one-sentence utterance, particularly if it was something simple like 'what time this afternoon's lecture begins'. But it is only for uncomplicated, bare facts about the world that the simple traditional model of comprehension will do. And indeed even at this basic level if I am firmly convinced that the lecture begins at five o'clock and I am only half-listening to what you say, I may be convinced that you *said* it was five o'clock even though you actually said it was to be at four o'clock: my previous belief so structures my expectations that these override the details of what you say. In considering the nature of comprehension then, we must expect that any extended discourse will be experienced differently by different listeners and they may have varying interpretations. Since we all have fluctuating attention, each listener may pay particular attention to a different part of the message and structure the rest of the message around what was, for that listener, the salient point.

But even beyond that, listeners who pay attention at the same moment, and agree on what was actually *said*, may disagree about what the speaker meant by what was said. If you are convinced that this politician really has the good of his constituents at heart and I am convinced that he has his own self-interest at heart, we will tend to interpret what he says in different ways—you as confirmation of your beliefs and I as confirmation of mine. If a friend and I meet a lecturer who has just been marking our exams and she says 'I really enjoyed reading your papers', my friend, who is an optimist, may take this as an indication of a good mark and I, who am a pessimist, may think she meant it sarcastically since I believe I wrote a poor paper. There is always a potential mismatch between the words the speaker uses and what the speaker meant by using those words.

Our normal experience of using our own language is that we achieve an adequate understanding of what the speaker said and what the speaker meant most of the time—occasionally later experience shows that actually we got it wrong to some degree. Communication is a risky business. Speakers know when they launch into speech that they may be misunderstood, indeed there may be some sorts of close relationships where the speaker may feel that there is no possibility of not being misunderstood. However, in spite of the fact that we normally achieve only partial success with our own utterances and must expect only partially to understand the language addressed to us, we manage our everyday lives in the expectation of sufficient mutual comprehension, a tolerable level of understanding. Obviously we have evolved a sufficient level of mutual comprehension as a species to have ensured our survival at least until the moment you are reading this—but we all know there are risks involved. This common-sense, everyday view of comprehension as being partial must surely be the view that we want our students to develop of comprehension in English. They should not expect or be expected to attain 100 per cent 'correct' comprehension. There is no such thing. One of the most damaging effects of testing is that it operates in terms of such expectations. At least in our teaching we should try to avoid this view. It instils a panic in students struggling with a foreign language. We should, rather, delightedly encourage groping towards some sort of comprehension which is tolerably consonant with our own.

1.2.2 The processes of comprehension

The view of the processes of comprehension which was developed during the 1940s and 1950s and which dominated EFL teaching for decades assumed that comprehension was built up from the bottom. You start off with recognizing phonetic sounds, you identify these as phonemes, you sort out the morphological structure—identify plural endings and so on—and so you arrive at a word. Then you undertake the same procedure for the next word and eventually you identify a phrase, say a noun phrase, and so you continue, building up structures until you have a sentence. You then interpret the sentence and come up with a semantic reading which will yield 'a thin meaning', and you then look at this in terms of the pragmatic context which will yield 'a thick meaning', which will include, for instance, what you think the speaker meant by what he or she said.

We now know that this simple model, 'the bottom up' model, is insufficient on its own. It has been repeatedly demonstrated that if listeners are presented with little bits of words on tape and asked to identify the consonants and vowels that these bits are composed of, they cannot do it. They perceive an acoustic blur without sufficient structure to enable them to recognize what it is they are listening to. Some researchers have shown that even chunks of sliced-off speech consisting of several syllables (indeed several 'words') may not be identified by native speakers. Equally, on the other hand, it has been shown that listeners perfectly well understand taped speech from which details of segments, even syllables, have been excised and replaced by, for instance, 'white noise', as long as they are given sufficient speech to understand. (This will not surprise someone who reads Chapter 4 of this book.)

It is clear that listeners are not simply passive processors who undertake automatic signal recognition exercises as acoustic signals are fed into them and so construct 'a meaning'. To begin with, as we have just shown, the signals they receive in human speech are frequently so debased that a signal-recognition processor simply does not have adequate data to work on, and cannot even get started. And yet human listeners do manage pretty well to identify what someone has said. How? The answer is that humans are active searchers for meaning. As soon as someone begins to speak, the co-operative human listener is actively trying to work out what he is saying, what he is likely to say next and what he is likely to mean by what he says. The active listener will use all relevant background knowledge— knowledge of the physical context of the utterance (the immediate surroundings, the place, the time of day, etc.), knowledge of the speaker (gender, age, known opinions), knowledge of the topic (and what the speaker is likely to know about it, or feel about it), and so on. Armed with all this activated knowledge the listener monitors the incoming acoustic signal, which will simultaneously shape and confirm his expectations.

A crucial part of the comprehension processes is this 'top down' processing, in which the listener actively marshalls previous knowledge in interpreting what is being said, as it is being said, so that prediction and interpretation have to be seen as interlinked processes which cannot be separated. Teachers often exploit this view of comprehension, trying to set up rich contexts for listening, contexts which will themselves activate any relevant knowledge that the foreign learner can bring to bear in trying to achieve an interpretation. This is without doubt an essential part of good teaching practice.

However, a problem for the foreign learner of a language still lies at the phonetic level. Even if you do manage to develop a rich set of predictions you still need to be able to monitor the incoming acoustic signal so that you know which of your predictions is being confirmed and which is not. You do need to be able to use all the phonetic cues that a native speaker takes for granted. You need to be able to use what segmental cues there are and to recognize how they are likely to be distributed in the acoustic continuum—this is the question addressed by Chapter 2. You also need to be able to use the information provided by the regular saliencies of speech, which draws your attention to the bits of language which the speaker is treating as crucial to the message. This is discussed in Chapter 3. Chapter 4 describes the ways in which the non-salient pieces of speech are typically simplified so that words often take on a form which is very different from that represented in a pronouncing dictionary. Chapter 5 draws attention to various functions of intonation in structuring messages and Chapter 6 describes some of the vocal features which may reveal what the speaker means by what he or she says. All of these chapters are intended to draw attention to cues which exist in the acoustic output of the speaker, which the listener needs to learn to use in a systematic fashion in monitoring what the speaker says. The final chapter discusses some of the implications of this for trying to *teach*, rather than test, listening comprehension.

1.3 The accent of English described in this book

The accent of English described here is that which is known in British phonetics literature as 'RP'—'received pronunciation'. This is the obvious accent to choose for several reasons—it is the only accent of which several segmental and intonational descriptions are readily available (cf. Gimson, 1962; Jones, 1962; Quirk *et al.*, 1973; Roach, 1983; Wells, 1982), it is the accent which is most usually taken as a model for foreign students and, finally, it is the accent towards which many educated speakers of other accents tend. Let me explain more fully what I mean by this last point. RP was, in the early years of the century, very narrowly interpreted. It applied only to speakers of 'Oxford' or 'BBC' English and often implied not only certain phonetic vowel and consonant qualities but also a certain very distinctive 'upper class' voice quality. Today it is more widely interpreted. Someone whose vowel qualities differ slightly from those described by Daniel Jones will still be said to speak with an RP accent if his vowels are distributed like those of RP—if he uses a given vowel that is quite like an RP vowel in the same set of words that other RP speakers use this vowel in. If a speaker from the north of England has in his speech vowels quite like the RP vowels in *ant* and *aunt* but he pronounces *past* and some similarly spelt words with the vowel like that in RP *ant* rather than that in *aunt* he will not be said to speak with an RP accent. If, however, because of social or other pressures, he learns to 'redistribute' these vowels to conform with a typical RP distribution he will then be said, in this wider usage, to 'speak RP'. Many teachers in universities and colleges and speakers on radio and television speak with an RP accent in this sense—their vowel and consonant qualities are quite like traditional RP qualities and they are distributed as in RP rather than in some other English accent. No doubt some people would prefer to restrict the term RP to its original narrow confines. I think it is more meaningful today to expand the term to include what might be called 'educated southern English'. Most of the examples in the earlier chapters of this book are taken from radio and television broadcasts. All examples of types of simplification in informal speech are types which occur regularly on BBC radio news broadcasts. I have imposed this lower bound of formality because it seems to me that everyone knows what he expects from such a style of delivery. For students using a British model of English, this is the most reasonable starting-point.

2 'Ideal' segments, syllables and words

In this chapter I shall describe in some detail the consonants and vowels of English and how they combine into syllables and into words. I shall describe them as they would be pronounced in their clearest and most explicit form; later, in describing some of the characteristics of informal speech, I shall speak of these as diverging from the maximally explicit, 'ideal' forms.

I have paid particular attention in the description to features which are often not made salient in conventional descriptions, for instance the fact that /f/ when pronounced in English *looks* different from /f/s pronounced in many neighbouring European languages. Also to points which, in my experience, teachers of English often find confusing and confused—like what 'voiced' and 'voiceless' consonants sound like in different phonetic contexts in English: I have tried to show whereabouts in the stream of speech the identifying features of voicing in voiced consonants are typically found. This is a characteristic of the general strategy in this chapter. It is not primarily concerned with giving a good and full description of how a particular sound is articulated by a speaker. What it is concerned to do is to draw attention to any visual cues which are regularly (or even frequently) present and which characterize a segment or a class of segments, also to striking auditory cues which it would be helpful for the teacher to draw the student's attention to. It is an account of pronunciation viewed not from the stance of the speaker but from the stance of the listener, and particularly of the listener who has the opportunity of *watching* the speaker speak. It is immensely helpful for most listeners to see the speaker's face as the speaker is talking. (It is well known that skilled deaf, or partially deaf, lip-readers can derive an extraordinary amount of information from carefully watching the speaker's lips, jaw, tongue when visible, as well as larger muscular movements which indicate the placing of stress and the patterning of intonation.) Students learning a foreign language need to be helped to use all the cues available to them.

2.1 The phoneme

It is well known that the orthographic form of a word may not always correspond directly with the sequence of segments which is heard when the word is spoken aloud. Thus for example the initial consonant in *no, know* and *gnome* is *n* in each case despite the orthographic variety. On the other hand *boot* and *foot* are pronounced with different vowels despite the orthographic similarity. However, for any given accent of English it is possible to construct a *phonemic transcription*, in which the same sound is always represented by the same symbol. For our examples *no, know* and *gnome* the phonemic transcription would be /nəʊ/, /nəʊ/ and /nəʊm/ respectively. Similarly *boot* will be transcribed /but/, where the /u/ represents the same vowel that is heard in *through*, whereas *foot* will be transcribed /fʊt/ which contains the vowel that occurs in the rhyming word *put*.

Teachers of spoken English are quite familiar with the idea of the phoneme and are accustomed to turning to pronouncing dictionaries using a phonemic transcription when they are in doubt about the pronunciation of a word. The idea of 'the same sound' is not usually a difficult one. Vowels can be tested to see whether or not they rhyme and the English orthography already predisposes us to accept the idea that the same consonant can appear in different places in a word as in *pip, tot* and *noon*.

It is important to realize that the notion 'the same sound' is an abstract notion and not one that can be physically demonstrated. If instrumental recording of a number of people's pronunciation of the vowel in *oh* are examined, it will be found that there is a considerable difference in the acoustic signal. Furthermore there is nothing in the acoustic signal which will uniquely identify this vowel as the vowel in *oh* and no other. If the same group of people now pronounce the words *coat, load* and *home,* which all have the 'same' vowel, the acoustic signals will be found to be even more widely divergent. Even if one individual pronounces this set of words, it will still be found that there is nothing in the acoustic, physical signal which will uniquely identify the vowel in these words as the 'same' vowel. It is not until a native speaker of the language identifies the vowels as the 'same' that they can be grouped together into the same phoneme. What the native speaker means by the 'same' is that he will allow these various acoustic signals to be acceptable tokens of the same basic type. In just the same way in our everyday lives we may handle many coins of a given value—the coins will have individual differences— they may be scratched, deformed, shiny and new, almost worn away, differing in absolute weight and size, differing in the date of their manufacture and perhaps in their design, but we still accept them, without even looking at them, as acceptable tokens of the basic type *ten pence piece.* The important point, with sounds and coins alike, is that they should be accepted as the 'same' in the community that is using them.

In their everyday informal speech, native speakers of English produce many sounds that they would regard as exotic and perhaps impossible to pronounce if confronted with in a foreign language. A sound rather like that at the end of German *ach* for example occurs very frequently—even in slow colloquial English—following a stressed vowel as in *working, sacking* or *marker.* When English native speakers come to learn a language in which such a sound occurs as a separate phoneme they tend to hear it, to begin with at least, as a token of /k/.

Speakers of all languages produce a far wider range of different phonetic sounds than phonemic descriptions would suggest. It is this phonetic overlap between languages—where very similar, even identical, phonetic sounds have to be interpreted as different phonemic tokens—which causes a great deal of difficulty in the teaching of the spoken form of a foreign language. In many languages of the world—for example, Cantonese or Luganda—the differences which hold pronunciations of /l/ and /r/ apart for English native speakers are quite unimportant. They are as unimportant as the posture of the lips, open or closed, at the beginning of the initial /k/ in *kick* for an English native speaker. For speakers of these languages our phonetically various [l]s and [r]s are tokens of the same phoneme, the 'same' sound. It is extremely difficult for speakers of these languages to distinguish between the different phonetic sounds that we produce in *lead* and *read* and *play* and *pray.* There are four phonetically distinct sounds here (/l/ and /r/ are pronounced without voicing following /p/) which speakers of these languages are used to accepting as tokens of one phoneme—but in order to control spoken English they have to learn to distinguish between them and assign two phonetically dissimilar sounds to an /l/ phoneme and the other two phonetically dissimilar sounds to an /r/ phoneme.

Where there is no phonetic overlap between a sound in one language and any sound in another, where one language has a sound that is really exotic to a student from the other language, the student rarely has any difficulty in perceiving the sound though he may have difficulty in producing it. Thus for instance speakers of English rarely have difficulty in perceiving the very retroflex sounds of South

Indian languages made with the tongue tip curled up and back, but the slightly retroflex sounds of North Indian languages are much more difficult to distinguish since phonetic sounds very like them can occur in normal English speech.

The ability to perceive phonetic sounds as tokens of one phoneme rather than another is also limited by the possible combinations of phonemes in the speaker's language and by his knowledge of what words are possible in his language. Suppose a native English speaker hears, in the middle of a sentence, a word that sounds as if it begins with /l/, then has the vowel in *lark*, and finally the consonant at the end of *sing*—/lɑŋ/. He knows there is no word *larng* in English, he may even at some sub-conscious level be aware that the phoneme /ɑ/ never precedes the consonant at the end of *sing*, so he must choose either *long* or *lung* as the word which is intended, and in this of course he will be guided by the context of the sentence and its syntax. Just as the English speaker finds it difficult to distinguish the vowels in *cup* and *carp* when they occur before /ŋ/ in a foreign language, so the Greek or Slavic speaker finds it difficult to distinguish between English /s/ and /z/ when they occur word finally, and for the same reason. The difference between the pronunciation of /s/ and /z/ does not distinguish between word shapes in Greek and Slavic languages in word final position. It must not be supposed, then, that because the native speaker of a given language will assign two phonetically different sounds to two different phonemes when they occur in one context, that he will necessarily preserve the same distinction in another context.

So far we have considered the 'abstract' nature of the phoneme from two related points of view. Firstly we considered the wide variety of physical signals that might be assigned to one phoneme and then we went on to think about some of the implications of viewing the phonemic system of a language as a system proper to each native speaker of the language, which each individual matches any given message to. When we come to considering the nature of a *phonemic description* of a language we find we need to develop our discussion of abstraction even further. Just what are we describing in a phonemic description? We are describing a phonological system which enables speakers of a language to communicate with each other. The only way we can begin to describe this phonological system which resides in the brains of the members of the speech community, is by observing the units of the system, the phonemes, as they are physically realized, as they are pronounced. But we have already said that the instrumental examination of the 'same' sound spoken by different individuals and in different contexts will not yield a unique set of characteristics by which we can unhesitatingly identify all the examples as examples of the 'same' sound. Clearly the physical characteristics of individuals, the size and configuration of larynx, tongue, palatal arch, cheeks, lips, to mention only a few relevant features, will profoundly affect the character of the acoustic signal. Similarly the manner of delivery, the speed, the physical circumstances of the individual—whether he has a cold or not, whether his mouth is full or not, whether he is drunk or not—will affect the acoustic signal. In order to describe the system of communication which is common to a speech community peopled with individuals of different physical characteristics and circumstances, we must ignore these individual variables. We must ignore a great deal of the physical message and try to abstract those variables which are common to the majority of members of the speech community in producing tokens of each phoneme. The easiest way to describe these in a way comprehensible to others is by selecting certain physical variables whose behaviour we can observe. We select the smallest number of articulatory variables which will enable us to characterize each phoneme and distinguish it from all the others. Notice how very far away we are from describing a *sound*. No measurable information is given about rate of movement of the articulators, degree of constriction or even the precise place of constriction. Only terms particular enough to keep each phoneme separate from the others are employed. Only movements which primarily contribute to the identification of the phoneme concerned are mentioned—there is no description of the posture or movement of any of the other articulators. Though it is clear, for instance, that the sides of the tongue must be in some relation to the upper and lower molars and that this relation will affect the resonance of any sound, since this relation of the sides of the tongue and the teeth and gums is crucial only in the identification of /l/, we ignore it for the identification of all other phonemes.

A further point needs to be made. We speak of making a *phonemic description*. In making such a description we isolate each phoneme and hold it, as it were, under the magnifying lens. This is yet another exercise in abstraction. It is clear that no native speaker of English walks around uttering tokens of phonemes in isolation. In describing the pronunciation of a phoneme we have to exercise a 'willing suspension of disbelief'. We have to pretend that we can freeze the articulation of a phoneme at some central point and that this central point will be representative of most pronunciations of the phoneme. (Any striking variant can be dealt with under the heading 'important allophone'.) We have to ignore the fact that any one realization of any phoneme will be different from any realization in a different environment. We have to ignore the fact that there are no determinable boundaries to a phonetic 'sound', that the acoustic signal is a continuum in which each realization of each sequential phoneme flows into the next. We have to ignore the fact that the only way we can identify the consonants in *pip, tit, kick,* by hearing alone, is by attending to the shape of the medial vowel.

One last point. It should be clear that, in order to make a phonemic description, we need to hear a token of each phoneme pronounced in short, clearly enunciated words. Then we describe the 'ideal' frozen posture of the phoneme as it is articulated with maximum clarity with all its characteristic features fully present. We need to have a form such as slow colloquial in order to be able to arrive at a phonemic description. It is quite impossible to make a phonemic transcription of normal informal speech. The number of phonemes grows so rapidly that the investigator finds himself quite unable to assign odd scraps of acoustic mess to a phoneme on any rational basis. The only basis on which he can do it is to require the speaker to repeat a form—and the repeatable form will be much clearer and slower, much more like slow colloquial. Every form, produced by every native speaker, no matter how informally and indistinctly pronounced, can be repeated by the speaker in a maximally clear way, in a slow colloquial style.

In describing the phonemes of English we rely on all these ideas of abstraction. We pretend to 'freeze' each phoneme as if a stable posture was maintained during its articulation. We pretend that a phoneme can be described independently of its context, of the phonemes on either side of it. We pretend that a phoneme can be physically identified by describing only those articulatory attributes which distinguish it from all other phonemes. We pretend that these articulatory attributes will be present in all instances of the pronunciation of the phoneme by all members of the speech community.

In the sections that follow I shall give a brief overview of the phonemic structure of English. I shall make a clear distinction between the *phonemic* classification, where we discuss the abstract units of the system of communication of a speech community, and the possible *phonetic* realizations of these abstract units. It is important to remember that the symbols used to represent phonemes, and the three-term labels used to characterize phonemes, are not phonetic descriptions. On the contrary, they are merely mnemonic devices to remind us of the general class of phonetic segments which these phonemes will be realized by. We would need much more information than this for a phonetic description. Consider /s/ which is characterized in many descriptions of English as a 'voiceless alveolar fricative'. This gives us very little specific indication of the phonetic character of an [s] which is very complex and involves, crucially, the formation of a groove or slit down the centre of the tongue while the sides of the tongue form a closure with the teeth and gums. If you simply release a [t], drawing the tongue slightly down and keeping it *flat*, you will produce a 'voiceless alveolar fricative' that is articulatorily and acoustically quite different from [s].

Since the characterization of an abstract phoneme is not the same as the phonetic description of a phonetic segment, I shall not feel bound to follow the conventional arrangements of pronunciation manuals in discussing classes of phonemes. I shall group phonemes together into classes which are determined by the way in which they function in English. We shall find that the phonetic segments which realize these classes will indeed have phonetic features in common, but in general we shall not need to identify such specific features as are needed in the discussion of pronunciation teaching. Thus at the phonemic level we shall not distinguish between 'bi-labial' and 'labio-dental' consonants since this distinction is not relevant at the phonemic level. At the phonemic level, where we are concerned with discussing the patterning of phonemes, all we need to know is whether a phoneme is 'labial' or not. At the phonetic level it is of course extremely important to know that the initial consonant in *pew* is bi-labial and that in *few* labio-dental—and of course we need a great deal more phonetic information than just that. The reader who would like more detailed phonetic information is referred to Gimson (1970). The phonological approach offered here owes more to Chomsky and Halle (1968)—that is to say at the phonological level I am more concerned with the patterning of phonemes than with the detail of their phonetic realization, and I believe that our knowledge of the patterns significantly affects the way in which we perceive phonetic detail.

2.2 The consonants of English

It is possible to identify each consonant by stating three facts about it:

(a) whereabouts in the mouth it is produced
(b) what sort of articulatory posture it is formed by
(c) what is happening in the larynx—is the consonant 'voiceless' or 'voiced'.

Rather than describe each consonant separately, I shall describe the features that identify sets of consonants. In the following table the consonants are arranged into rows and columns. Each row and each column have some articulatory feature in common.

Only /h/ does not share any classificatory features with any other consonant. Each column contains a set of consonants that have in common the fact that they are produced in the same part of the mouth. Rows 1 (and 1i) to 4 contain sets of consonants that are formed by similar articulatory postures. Rows 1 and 2 contain consonants that differ from those in rows 1i and 2i by being voiceless as opposed to voiced. I shall describe the features shared by each column and each row. I am aware that this may produce some practical difficulties. It is impossible, in this presentation, to look up a phoneme and find all its identifying features discussed under one heading. The advantage of this presentation on the other hand is that it is possible to show the quite general patterns of similarity between different classes of phonemes without repeating the information several times over in the discussion of individual phonemes. Also we shall find the format of this table useful when we come on to discussing syllable and word structure later (section 2.4). I hope the advantages will outweigh the disadvantages.

TABLE 1

	A	B	C	D	E	F
1	p	t		tʃ	k	
1i	b	d		dʒ	g	
2	f	θ	s	ʃ		
2i	v	ð	z	ʒ		
3	m	n			ŋ	
4	w	l	r	j		
5						h

Under each heading I shall discuss the general feature which is shared by members of a column or row. Then I shall point out any special way in which this feature is realized in the pronunciation of each phoneme. I shall mention not only the interior arrangements of the articulatory tract but also any visual feature which may be relied on as an identificatory signal. Where pronunciation of the English feature raises few or no difficulties for foreign learners the description is very brief. Where the identificatory phonetic features of English differ from those of several foreign languages in a striking way, I shall comment on these differences. It is important to make a clear distinction, in this context, between phonological and phonetic entities. Whereas many languages may possess a phoneme that may be phonemically transcribed as /f/ in the phonemic inventory of the language, this does not mean that the phonetic features which identify /f/ will be identical in all these languages. As we shall see in our discussion of the formation of English /f/, it is articulated in a way which is strikingly different from the /f/s of most other European languages. Similarly the phonemic pair /p/, /b/ exists in many languages. The way in which these phonemes are to be identified phonetically differs from one language to another and, again, the realization of this pair in English is very different from that of many other languages. We shall pursue this in 2.2.3. The general point to note here is that the fact of two languages each possessing a phoneme transcribed by the same phonemic symbol, and called by the same phonemic name, must not be taken to mean that these phonemes are pronounced with identical phonetic identifying features.

In the descriptive sections which follow I shall pass over well known and well described aspects very rapidly. The reader who would like more detailed description of these points is referred to Gimson (1970).

2.2.1 Place of articulation

The first column, column A, contains the following phonemes /p, b, m, f, v, w/. All of these phonemes share the feature that the bottom lip is primarily involved in its articulation. These consonants are all *labial* consonants. /p, b, m/ are all formed by closing the lower lip against the upper lip. /w/ is formed by pushing forward the corners of the mouth and wrinkling the lips so that a small rounded central aperture is formed while simultaneously raising the back of the tongue towards the roof of the mouth. /p, b, m/ rarely prove articulatorily difficult. /f/ and /v/ however are pronounced in a way rather different from the /f/ and /v/ of many other languages. The upper teeth bite into the soft *inside* of the lower lip. In most other European languages the upper teeth bite either on to the *top* of the lower lip or even on to the *outside* of the lower lip. The visual impression is quite different. In those languages where the teeth bite on to the top or the outside of the lower lip, there is a clear view of the lower edges of the upper teeth during the articulation. In English the lower edges of the upper teeth are quite obscured by the lower lip.

The second column, column B, contains the following consonants:

/t, d, n, θ, ð, l/. All these consonants are formed by a stricture between the tongue tip or blade and the dental ridge or back of the
upper teeth. In forming these consonants the tongue tip forms a stricture either with the back of the upper teeth or with the dental (also
called alveolar) ridge. We shall call this set *dental/alveolar*. /t, d, n/
are pronounced with the tongue tip or blade making a closure against
the dental ridge, the area immediately behind the upper teeth. The
area of contact between the tongue tip or blade and the dental ridge
is very narrow. This is quite unlike the pronunciation of /t/ and /d/
in many languages where the tip of the tongue forms a closure right
up against the back of the upper teeth, and the blade of the tongue
continues the closure against the dental ridge. This extensive closure
results in a very much 'thicker' sound than that which is produced
by the relatively small area of closure in the pronunciation of these
consonants in English. /θ/ and /ð/ are pronounced with the tongue
tip forming a stricture just behind the upper teeth. These consonants
are frequently taught to foreign students as interdental consonants,
with the tongue tip actually showing between the front teeth during
the articulation. There are obvious pedagogical advantages in this,
in that the teacher can see that the student is making a gesture
towards the teeth rather than the dental ridge. There are however
disadvantages in that the big forward movement of the tongue tends
to slow up the articulation of words containing these consonants. Also
when foreign teachers of English retain this habit in their own
speech, they accustom their students to a visual clue which they will
be denied in watching native English speakers talking. The last consonant /l/ is formed by making a tongue tip closure, as for /d/,
against the dental ridge but lowering one or both sides of the tongue
so that the air can flow over the side(s) of the tongue.

The third column, C, contains only three consonants, /s, z, r/.
All these involve complex articulations with the tip or blade of the
tongue opposed to some part of the dental ridge. All three involve
the blade of the tongue being pulled down to form a cupped area
with the sides and tip of the tongue forming the rim of the cup. This
is not a class which can be easily characterized. However in order to
identify this set I shall call it *post-dental*.

Column D contains the consonants /tʃ, dʒ, ʃ, ʒ, j/. Since they
all involve articulation further back in the oral cavity than any we
have yet encountered I shall identify them as *palatal*. It is a marked
feature of the first four of these consonants that many speakers have
strong pouting-out of the lips during their articulation. The corners
of the mouth are pushed strongly forward and the lower lip may be

so markedly pouted that the soft inner surface of the lip is visible. The lip movement on these consonants is more marked than on any other English sounds, including the so-called 'rounded' vowels.

Column E contains /k, g, ŋ/. All these consonants are formed with the back of the tongue making a closure against the soft palate or velum. These consonants are called *velar*.

Column F contains only /h/. English /h/ must not, as in some languages which have a phoneme symbolized by /h/, be considered as primarily a glottal or pharyngeal fricative. It is rather a voiceless breathy onset to the following vowel. Thus if the articulation of /h/ in *he* and *hard* is prolonged it will be found in each case to have the resonance of the following vowel. There may be a little local friction, appropriate to the following vowel, when the vowel is formed by the tongue being close to the roof of the mouth as in *he* and *hue*.

2.2.2 Manner of articulation

We shall look along the rows of consonants in Table 1 as we discuss the manner of articulation, the articulatory posture which characterizes the pronunciation of a consonant.

Rows 1 and 1i contain the consonants /p, t, tʃ, k, b, d, dʒ, g/. All of these consonants are formed by a complete obstruction of the airstream so that no air escapes while the closure is maintained either through the mouth or into the nasal cavities. There is a *velic closure*, a raising of the soft palate to prevent air entering the nasal cavities during the pronunciation of these consonants, as well as an *oral closure*. The oral closure is as we have seen, *labial* in the case of /p/ and /b/, *alveolar* in the case of /t/ and /d/ and so on.

/p, t, k, b, d, g/ are called *stops* or *plosives*.
/tʃ/ and /dʒ/ are called *affricated stops*.

This distinction is made because in the pronunciation of /tʃ/ and /dʒ/ the stop period is relatively short, shorter than it is for the other stops, and the release of the closure is very gradual giving rise to a strongly fricative sound.

Rows 2 and 2i contain the consonants /f, θ, s, ʃ, v, ð, z, ʒ/. During the pronunciation of a fricative there is no complete obstruction of the airstream as there is in a stop, but one articulator is placed so close to another as to interfere with the passage of air. This yields the characteristic 'hissing', 'hushing' or 'buzzing' sound that one associates with fricatives. The obstructing articulator causes turbulence of the airstream just as the presence of a large number of rocks in a rapidly flowing river gives rise to turbulence in the current. The description *fricative* does however better describe some members of this set of consonants than others. Even in slow colloquial pronunciation some fricatives sound much more fricative than others. All the consonants in row 2 sound more fricative than /v/ and /ð/. This is because in the pronunciation of the consonants in row 2 the obstruction which causes the friction is assailed by the unobstructed airstream from the lungs. For the consonants in row 2i on the other hand there has already been some obstruction at the larynx as the airstream passes through the narrowed and vibrating glottis.

The fricatives in the first two columns, /f, v, θ, ð/ sound much less fricative than those in columns C and D. /s, z, ʃ, ʒ/ are often referred to as *sibilant* fricatives because of the particularly high pitched friction associated with them.

We can rank the fricatives on a scale of 'sounding more fricative' to 'sounding less fricative' in the following order:

/s, ʃ, z, ʒ, f, θ, v, ð/.

/v/ and /ð/ are frequently pronounced, even in slow colloquial pronunciation, with no audible friction.

Row 3 contains the nasal consonants /m, n, ŋ/. For each of them the place of articulation is exactly that of the homorganic stop in their own columns. Thus /m/ is articulated at the lips like /p/ and /b/ and so on. Whereas the stops have a *velic closure*, a raising of the velum which prevents air resonating in the nasal cavities, during the articulation of *nasal* consonants the velum is lowered thus allowing air to pass into the nasal cavities and set up resonance there.

Row 4 contains a set of consonants that are called by a wide variety of names, and they are indeed an assorted set. I shall refer to them as *approximants*. They share the characteristics of being realized neither by complete obstruction of the airstream (as in a stop) nor by such partial obstruction as causes a turbulence of the airstream (as in a fricative) but by a much more vowel-like articulation, in which it is clear where the place of maximum modification of the airstream is located in the mouth. All of these sounds, if prolonged, sound like vowels. However, they must be classified as consonants in English because they behave like consonants—for instance they can all precede a vowel in the same syllable as in *wet, let, red* and *yet*, and in each case we can demonstrate that the form of the articles before words beginning with these phonemes is that appropriate to a consonant, not a vowel.

/w/ is formed by pushing forward the corners of the mouth and contracting the lips round a small central opening. Vertical lines appear on the surface of the lips. Simultaneously the back of the tongue is raised towards the soft palate.

/l/ is realized by a central closure of the blade of the tongue against the dental ridge and the lowering of one or both sides of the tongue to allow a lateral escape of the airstream. If the front of the tongue is raised simultaneously a 'clear' /l/ results—as in *low* where the /l/ sounds as though a close front vowel (like the one in *eat*) is being uttered *during* the /l/ articulation. 'Clear' /l/s occur in syllable initial position—the 'clearest' /l/ of all is in syllable initial position *and* immediately preceding a close front vowel, as in *leaf* or *lean*. 'Dark' /l/s occur syllable finally. During the articulation for the /l/ the back of the tongue is raised in the mouth giving to the /l/ the resonance of a back vowel like the one in *caw*. 'Dark' /l/s are especially 'dark' following back vowels as in *call* and *pull*.

/r/ can be realized in several markedly different ways. Initially, as in *rose* or *red*, it is formed with the tongue tip turned up towards the back of the dental ridge. No friction is heard in these words. When /r/ follows a consonant it may be slightly fricative as in *drive* and *tree*. The lips are pouted and the corners of the mouth pushed forward during the articulation. Following /θ/, as in *three*, and between vowels, as in *very* and *orange*, /r/ is sometimes realized as a quick

TABLE 2

	consonant (stop)	consonant (approximant)	vowel
indefinite article	a pet /ə pet/	a war /ə wɔ/	an oar /ən ɔ/
		a lot /ə lɒt/	an ear /ən ɪə/
		a room /ə rum/	
		a year /ə jɪə/	
definite article	the pet /ðə pet/	the war /ðə wɔ/	the oar /ðɪ ɔ/
		the lot /ðə lɒt/	the ear /ðɪ ɪə/
		the room /ðə rum/	
		the year /ðə jɪə/	

tap against the dental ridge—rather like a very fast [d]. This last variant is rare in younger RP speakers.

/j/ is formed with the hump of the tongue pushed up towards the hard palate but not pushed so far as to cause friction. The stricture is closest before front vowels so the /j/ in *yeast* for example is articulated with the front of the tongue more raised than it is in *yak*. All these consonants have a voiceless variant which may be slightly fricative when they follow 'voiceless' initial consonants as in *twist, play* and *free*.

The last row contains only /h/. /h/ is a 'loner' with a wide variety of realizations, all of them breathy onsets to following vowels. It is sometimes described as a fricative but is rarely fricative in English.

2.2.3 'Voicing' and 'voicelessness'

I have left this part of the description of consonants to last because it is the most difficult and the most widely misunderstood. In most descriptions of English (see especially Jones, 1962; Gimson, 1970) a distinction is made between *voiced* and *voiceless* consonants. Thus the consonants in Table 1 (p. 21) rows 1 and 2 are said to be *voiceless* (that is /p, t, tʃ, k, f, θ, s, ʃ/) and the corresponding consonants in rows 1i and 2i to be *voiced*. In reading such descriptions it is important to make a clear distinction between the general phonetic meaning of the terms voicing and voicelessness and the phonological meaning of the terms. I shall try to make clear how such a distinction is to be drawn.

In general phonetic terms a voiced segment is uttered with vibration of the vocal cords and a voiceless segment is uttered with the vocal cords apart, with no vibration of the vocal cords. You can test this general phonetic description by putting your fingers in your ears and saying a long [sssss] followed by a long [zzzzz]. During the [sssss] you should not perceive any buzzing resonating in your head, but during a voiced [zzzzz] there will be a quite remarkably loud buzzing in the head. In general phonetic terms the [sssss] will be said to be *voiceless* and the [zzzzz] to be *voiced*. Any recorded segment can be examined to see if there is vocal cord vibration during its articulation. If there is, it is said to be voiced, no matter what language it is taken from, no matter what its environment is. Voicing, then, in general phonetic terms is a physical property which can be stated of a particular stretch of acoustic signal with no access to any information about its language of origin, environment and so on.

Now it is perhaps a pity that these terms were ever used to describe the pronunciation of classes of phonemes in particular languages. (It is for this reason that some authorities have used the terms 'fortis' and 'lenis' rather than 'voiceless' and 'voiced', cf. Gimson, 1962, p. 32.) In English for example the term 'voiced stop' does not mean that in all positions and in all realizations such a consonant will be voiced. Let us consider the class of 'voiced stops' in English, /b, d, g/. In initial position there is no voicing during the closure for the stop. From a general phonetic point of view the segments initial in *boy, duck* and *gull* must be said to be voiceless. This is of course very confusing for speakers of Romance languages like Italian and French where their initial /b/, /d/ and /g/ are all from a general phonetic point of view 'voiced stops'.

The terms 'voiced' and 'voiceless' as used in the characterization of the consonants of English must be understood to be used to characterize classes of consonants that behave in a certain way—not to be a phonetic description of all realizations of all these consonants. I shall continue to use the terms 'voiceless' and 'voiced' to identify the sets of stops and fricatives in English since these are familiar terms. When I use them in this identifying, phonological sense, I shall surround them with inverted commas—'voiceless', 'voiced'. Since these terms are not, in fact, descriptive phonetic terms it is necessary to examine carefully what we mean by 'voiced' and 'voiceless' in different contexts.

The 'voiceless' stops

Consider the 'voiceless' stops in row 1 of Table 1—/p, t, k/. Initially in a stressed syllable, they are immediately followed by a puff of air which has the quality of the following approximant or vowel—this puff of air is called 'aspiration'. In the following examples, I shall attempt to show how the quality of the aspiration varies. In the first column I shall give the orthographic form of the word, in the second the phonemic form, and in the third a phonetic transcription in which the subscript [o] indicates the quality of the aspiration following the 'voiceless' stop:

pea	/pi/	[pii̥]
two	/tu/	[tu̥u]
core	/kɔ/	[kɔ̥ɔ]
please	/pliz/	[pl̥iz]
tray	/treɪ/	[tr̥eɪ]
quick	/kwɪk/	[kw̥ɪk]

It is this aspiration which chiefly distinguishes initial 'voiceless' stops from their 'voiced' counterparts.

In word final position all members of row 1 are distinguished by being preceded by a comparatively short vowel and glottalization. I include within the term *glottalization* both tenseness of the vocal cords, which may give rise to creakiness in the vowel, and closure of the glottis which forms a glottal stop. In forming a glottal stop, the vocal cords are brought together and closed, so that no air seeps through them. This complete closure necessarily has an effect on the type of vibration of the vocal cords immediately preceding it. The quality of voicing in vowels immediately preceding a glottal stop is 'tighter', more 'creaky' than the fully voiced voicing which precedes final 'voiced' stops. This difference is especially remarkable following the close front vowel /i/ as in *seat* and *seed*. The 'voiceless' stops and the affricate /tʃ/ are distinguished from their 'voiced' counterparts in word final position by being preceded by

(a) a relatively short vowel with 'tight' voicing
(b) a glottal stop.

In the following examples the dot under the vowel indicates that it is short and has 'tight' voicing and the symbol [ʔ] represents the glottal stop:

leap	/lip/	[liʔp]
pot	/pɒt/	[pɒ̣ʔt]
soak	/səʊk/	[sə̣ʊʔk]
catch	/kætʃ/	[kæ̣ʔtʃ]

In each case the vowel is chopped off abruptly by the closure for the glottal stop. Where the 'voiceless' stops follow a nasal or lateral, the nasal or lateral is shorter than it is before a 'voiced' consonant, as well as the vowel being shorter:

help	/help/	[hẹlʔp]
sent	/sent/	[sẹnʔt]
pinch	/pɪntʃ/	[pɪ̣nʔtʃ]
bulk	/bʌlk/	[bʌ̣lʔk]

Intervocalically before an unstressed syllable the 'voiceless' stops are not normally preceded by a glottal stop. They are very briefly, lightly articulated and are frequently not realized by a stop at all but by an articulation which just stops short of a stop. This would have to be described as a 'fricative' articulation in general phonetic terms but it is much less fricative than the articulation associated with segments symbolized [f], [s] etc. I shall therefore place an asterisk after the relevant symbols in the phonetically transcribed examples to indicate a segment that is either realized as a very lightly and briefly articulated stop or as an articulation which does not quite reach the position for complete closure:

tapping	/tapɪŋ/	[tap*ɪŋ]
writer	/raɪtə/	[raɪt*ə]
worker	/wɜkə/	[wɜk*ə]

The affricate /tʃ/ is normally pronounced with a very brief closure intervocalically, followed by friction.

The 'voiced' stops

Initially the 'voiced' stops are realized by a period of voiceless closure (i.e. no vibration of the vocal cords) with, as the closure is released, immediate onset of voicing in the following segment. The difference between initial 'voiceless' and 'voiced' stops lies, then, in the timing of onset of voicing immediately following the release of the closure. The behaviour of the vocal cords during the period of closure itself is no different. This is, of course, quite different from the case in French, for example, where there is vibration of the vocal cords during the period of closure.

I shall try to illustrate this difference by a diagram. ———— indicates closure. We shall consider the words *peat* and *beat* so that ———— represents, in the first place, closure at the lips and, finally, closure at the dental ridge. , , , , , indicates voicing:

```
peat ————               , , , , , , , , , , ?  ———————————
     p        i         i            i    ?              t
bead ————  , , , , , , , , , , , , , , , , , , , , , , , ,  ————
     b            i                  d
```

(The length of the line ____ indicates the comparative length of the periods of closure. All things being equal, 'voiceless' consonants have a longer period of constriction than 'voiced' ones, and initial ones are shorter than final ones. This is however a difficult variable to learn to perceive and bring under conscious control so we shall not discuss it further here.)

The point to notice is that the /p/ closure is released into a period of voiceless vowel (aspiration) whereas, as the /b/ closure is released, it is immediately followed by a voiced vowel. So the main difference in the following pairs lies in the different timing of the onset of voice:

palm	balm	/pɑm/	/bɑm/	[pɑ̥ɑm]	[pɑm]
tin	din	/tɪn/	/dɪn/	[tɪ̥ɪn]	[tɪn]
con	gone	/kɒn/	/gɒn/	[kɒ̥ɒn]	[kɒn]

I have tried, by this somewhat controversial phonetic transcription, to indicate that the distinction between the initial segment in each pair lies not in the period of closure but in what immediately *follows* the period of closure. The fact that two symbols are used following the 'voiceless' stop should not be taken to indicate that the vowel element is longer in these words than in those containing the 'voiced' stop—it is not.

The same distinction holds in 'voiceless' versus 'voiced' initial clusters:

plight	blight	/plaɪt/	/blaɪt/	[pl̥aɪt]	[plaɪt]
trunk	drunk	/trʌŋk/	/drʌŋk/	[tr̥ʌŋk]	[trʌŋk]
crow	grow	/krəʊ/	/grəʊ/	[kr̥əʊ]	[krəʊ]

Having made the point that the difference between 'voiceless' and 'voiced' initial stops lies in the timing of the onset of voice in the next segment rather than in the period of closure, I shall now revert to a more conventional phonetic transcription.

I have dealt at some length with the initial 'voiced'/'voiceless' distinction in stops, in a sense unnecessarily so, since this is a well-known characteristic of English and in any case no misunderstandings are likely to arise if voicing does appear in initial 'voiced' closures—after all in some native accents of England, Yorkshire for example, such voicing is frequently found.

A much more important point to dwell upon, since this is not usually stressed in manuals of English pronunciation and it is consequently often unknown to foreign teachers of English, is the way the word *final* distinction between 'voiceless' and 'voiced' stops is made. The main distinction is between a relatively short vowel, with 'tight' voicing and glottal stop preceding a 'voiceless' stop, and a relatively long vowel with 'full' voicing preceding a 'voiced' stop. Let us consider for a moment the pair *seat* and *seed*. We shall ignore the beginning of the word and concentrate on the end:

```
seat   s , , , , , , , ,       t
       s         i             t
seed   s , , , , , , , , , , , , , d
       s         i                 d
```

The vowel in *seat* is quite short and chopped off abruptly by the glottal stop. The voicing in the vowel is 'tight' and is represented by [,]. In *seed* the voicing is full and continues unabated into the closure. The vowel is very much longer than that in *seat*. (This demonstrates the fact that the much used terms 'short' and 'long' to designate classes of English vowels can be misleading since here the same vowel phoneme /i/ is realized in *seat* as a relatively 'short' vowel and in *seed* as a long vowel.)* Let us now turn to what happens during the closure and release phases of /t/ and /d/ respectively in these words. There is voicelessness during the closure for /t/ and, if the closure is audibly released, it is released into a tiny voiceless central vowel [si?t³]. For /d/ some speakers will have a dying away of voicing, some 'whisper' during the beginning of the closure, for others there will be no voicing at all during the closure. /d/, like /t/, will be released, if it is audibly released, into a voiceless central vowel. This is a very important point to note since many foreign (and indeed many native English) teachers tend to demonstrate a final 'voiced' stop in English by releasing it into a voiced central vowel— /'sid ³/. This form only occurs in very unusual situations in English—as for example where someone wishes to draw attention to the ending of a word — 'I said sea*t* (['si?tə]) not *seed* (['sidə])'. It never occurs in normal speech. The main distinction between 'voiceless' and 'voiced' stops in word final position lies in the realization of the preceding vowel—not in the articulation of the stop itself or of its release. It is thus quite parallel to the distinction between 'voiceless' and 'voiced' stops in initial position where, as we have seen, the distinction lies not in the closure of the stop itself but in the timing of onset of voicing in the segments following release of the closure. Let us examine some pairs of words differing in the 'voicing' of the final stop. In each case we show them with final release:

cup	cub	/kʌp/	/kʌb/	[kʌ?p³]	[kʌːᵇp³]
kit	kid	/kɪt/	/kɪd/	[kɪ?t³]	[kɪːᵈt³]
knack	nag	/næk/	/næg/	[næ?k³]	[næːᵍk³]

([ː] marks length on the vowel before the 'voiced' consonants.) Again I have used a rather controversial phonetic transcription to try to bring home the point that the distinction between these two sets of stops in final position lies not in the final closure and its release but in the preceding vowel. In fact as this transcription suggests, there

---

* Those who use the 'short'–'long' classification wish to draw attention to the fact that in the *same phonetic context* /i/ will be realized as longer than /ɪ/, and /ɒ/ than /ɔ/. This is of course true. However, the unfortunate result of this is that many foreign learners interpret this as meaning (a) that a 'long' vowel is long in all phonetic contexts and (b) as meaning that 'short' vowels are equally short and 'long' vowels are equally long. In fact at least one of the 'short' vowels, /æ/ is regularly longer than /i/ in the same phonetic context, and some of the 'long' vowels, notably /ɔ/ are very much longer than other 'long' vowels in the same phonetic context.

will often be some whisper (very slight voicing) at the beginning of the closure for /b, d, g/. It does however clearly make the point that the crucial distinction that must be observed lies in the realization of the vowels preceding these sets of consonants.

The distinction between the final affricates /tʃ/ and /dʒ/ is realized like that between the stops in final position—the vowel preceding /tʃ/ in *catch* is shorter and has 'tighter' voicing than the vowel preceding /dʒ/ in *cadge*. Similarly the /tʃ/ is immediately preceded by a glottal stop which abruptly cuts off the vowel:

catch   cadge   /kætʃ/   /kædʒ/   [kæʔtʃ]   [kæːᵈtʃ]

Again this transcription is slightly misleading in that the closure for the affricate in *cadge* will have very slight voicing or whisper in it—but the final fricative element will not be voiced in either case.

In intervocalic position the terms 'voiceless' and 'voiced' which characterize the two sets of consonants in rows 1 and 2 can be interpreted in general phonetic terms. The distinction is between 'voiceless' /p, t, tʃ, k/ as in *capping, utter, catching, lacking*, and 'voiced' /b, d, dʒ/ and /g/ as in *cabby, udder, cadging* and *lagging*. The 'voiced' stops, like the 'voiceless' stops, tend to be articulated very lightly when intervocalic before an unstressed syllable—or indeed, like the 'voiceless' stops are realized by an articulation which falls just short of being a stop. In the following examples this 'weak' stop, or phonetic non-stop, is shown followed by [*]:

labour   /leɪbə/   [leɪb*ə]
seeding   /sidɪŋ/   [sid*ɪŋ]
wagging   /wægɪŋ/   [wæg*ɪŋ]

The fricatives
The fricatives, like the stops, are divided into sets which are frequently labelled 'voiceless' and 'voiced'.

| 'voiceless' | f | θ | s | ʃ | (row Z) |
| 'voiced' | v | ð | z | ʒ | (row Zi) |

Initially the main difference between the two sets is that the 'voiceless' member of each pair is realized as longer and more fricative than its 'voiced' congener. Thus in *fie, vie* and *thigh, thy* the initial /f/ and /θ/ are held longer and are more fricative than the comparatively non-fricative /v/ and /ð/ which are briefly and laxly articulated with little, if any, audible friction. The contrast between /s/ and /z/ as in *sip* and *zip* is even more striking as the relatively

long and hissing /s/ contrasts with the shorter, much less fricative,
/z/. There is of course no contrast between /ʃ/ and /ʒ/ initially since
/ʒ/ never occurs initially. /ʃ/ initially has strong 'hushing' friction.
The 'voiced' set may have whisper during the constriction which
develops into voice as the stricture opens into the following vowel.
The initial onset of the stricture is not voiced. Thus we might narrowly transcribe these 'voiced' fricative onsets thus:

veal	/vil/	[fviəl]
those	/ðəʊz/	[θðəʊz]
zoo	/zu/	[szu]

In this respect the 'voiced' fricatives are just like the 'voiced' stops—
there is never a voiced onset to the constriction in initial position.

In word final position the fricatives again have something in common with the stops. The main distinguishing feature of
'voicelessness' and 'voice' lies in the length of the preceding vowel.
There is of course no question of the 'voiceless' fricative being
preceded by 'tight' voicing and a glottal stop, but the vowel is still
comparatively short. Again there is more friction in the realization of
the 'voiceless' fricatives and they are longer than the 'voiced' ones.
There may be very slight voicing in the final 'voiced' fricatives but,
like the stops, they are released as phonetically voiceless—in the case
of the fricatives like voiceless fricatives. Thus the contrast *cease, seize*—
/sis/, /siz/ is not phonetically realized as [siːs], [siːzᵊ] as is
sometimes supposed, but as [sis], [siːzs]. Here are examples of the
fricative pairs:

safe	save	/seɪf/	/seɪv/	[seɪf]	[seɪːvf]
teeth	teethe (v.)	/tiθ/	/tið/	[tiθ]	[tiːðθ]
mace	maize	/meɪs/	/meiz/	[meɪs]	[meɪːzs]
rush	rouge	/rʌʃ/	/ruʒ/	[rʌʃ]	[ruːʒʃ]

Once again this transcription is slightly misleading in that it suggests
that *after* the long vowel one has to produce two consecutive segments
in order to articulate a 'voiced' fricative—in fact there is only one and
that is like a very weak version of the 'voiceless' fricative—certainly for
those students who have a tendency to produce a voiced vowel after
a final 'voiced' fricative a valuable exercise is to learn to expect a
'voiceless' fricative instead.

Intervocalically the main difference between the two sets of fricatives lies in the presence of voicing in the 'voiced' set and in the
greater friction in the 'voiceless' set.

2.3 The vowels of English

The vowels of English are dealt with very briskly in this section. This
is because a very complete and detailed description is available in
Gimson (1962). I am, however, going to take advantage of this short
section to mention in detail some points about specific vowels which
are sometimes overlooked by teachers of English. The following table
shows the vowel phonemes of English:

TABLE 3*

	A	B	C	D
1	ɪ	i	jʊ	ɪə
2	e	eɪ		eə
3	æ	aɪ	aʊ	ɑ
4	ɒ	ɔɪ	əʊ	ɔ
5	ʊ		u	ʊə
6	ʌ			
7	ə			ɜ

This table is not arranged according to the fine detail of phonetic
pronunciation. I have chosen to group together vowels which have a
similar distribution and they are arranged in classes whose members
behave in similar ways in the stream of speech (cf. 4.4).

Column A shows the basic vowel series, sometimes referred to as
the 'short' vowels, but since they are of varying lengths and (/æ/
especially) are frequently longer than some of the so-called 'long'
vowels, we shall not use these general categories here. The basic
vowel series is exemplified in the following words:

/ɪ/	pit
/e/	pet
/æ/	pat
/ɒ/	pot
/ʊ/	put
/ʌ/	putt/cut
/ə/	apart

* Where I wish to indicate that a diphthong is realized phonetically as long, I put
the length marker [ː] after the complete diphthongal symbol. This does not imply
that it is only the 'second part' of the diphthong which is lengthened, since I take
the diphthong to be an unanalysable whole during which the tongue is constantly
in motion. The length symbol indicates that the whole diphthong is lengthened
with the relative balance of weight over the diphthong remaining as it is in its
unlengthened form.

These vowels all share the distributional characteristic that none of them can appear in a stressed monosyllable that is not closed by a consonant—in all examples above, each stressed monosyllable is closed by the consonant /t/. The final vowel /ə/ can only occur in unstressed syllables. This series is also distinguished by the fact that the only vowels which can precede /ŋ/ appear in it—the vowels in *sing, sang, song* and *sung.* (There is also a rare occurrence of /e/ as in *length.*)

The only vowel of this series that I want to make a particular comment on is /æ/. It is not sufficiently realized that this vowel is quite long in modern English. It is strikingly longer than /ɪ/ or /e/, for instance. Before voiced consonants it is often diphthongized as in [bæəd], *bad.*

Column B shows the front closing vowels:

/i/	beat, bee
/eɪ/	bait, bay
/aɪ/	bite, buy
/ɔɪ/	boil, boy

The degree of closeness of the front closing depends on the degree of closeness of the first part of these complex segments. Thus the first vowel, /i/, may be equally close throughout, but /ɔɪ/ will end in a much more open quality. In all these vowels there is more weight in the first part than in the second and the tongue shape keeps on changing.

/i/ is a close, front, unrounded vowel, a good deal closer and more front that /ɪ/. It may sometimes be marginally longer than /ɪ/ but this is not a consistent feature and, compared with the other vowels in columns B, C and D, /i/ must be considered a 'short' vowel. Before a 'voiceless' consonant /i/ is realized as short and with unvarying quality. Before 'voiced' consonants and in open syllables, as in *bead, bee,* /i/ is realized with a diphthongal quality beginning from a more open position and rising to the close, front position.

In slow, explicit, 'idealized' speech, all of these vowels share the characteristic that, if they are immediately followed by another vowel the front closing is often realized as a slight [j] glide thus:

being	/biɪŋ/	[biʲɪŋ]
baying	/beɪɪŋ/	[beʲɪŋ]
buying	/baɪɪŋ/	[baʲɪŋ]
buoying	/bɔɪɪŋ/	[bɔʲɪŋ]

The closeness of stricture for the [j] depends on the closeness of the starting point of the vowel so it is closer following /i/ and more open following /aɪ/.

Column C contains the back closing vowels:

/ju/	cute, new
/aʊ/	shout, now
/əʊ/	boat, no
/u/	boot, do

/ju/ is treated as a single phonological unit in this description for two reasons. First, we find /ju/ functioning in morphological alternation to a single unit, /ʌ/, in pairs like *punitive* and *punish* (a relationship which is clearly borne out by the orthographic convention in this case) and in general, in morphologically unrelated pairs like *cute* /kjut/ and *cut* /kʌt/. Secondly, we find that the sequence /ju/ has a normal distribution for a vowel, in that it can occur following most consonants. If this item is analysed as consonant /j/ plus vowel /u/ we have to explain the curious distributional constraint which allows only the vowel /u/ to follow a sequence consonant plus /j/ as in *pew* /pju/, *few* /fju/ and *queue* /kju/. Why do we not find */kjɜ/, */pjɑ/, */fjɔ/?

/ju/ starts with the front of the tongue in a close position and then, like a wave, the front of the tongue is depressed and the back of the tongue rises to close position. The prominence is on the last element (which is why this is sometimes analysed as a sequence approximant /j/ + vowel /u/). The lips move from unrounded to close, rounded.

/u/ is a close, back, rounded vowel, closer and with the lips much more tightly rounded than /ʊ/. It may occasionally be longer but the qualitative difference of tongue height and lip posture is much more striking. Before 'voiceless' consonants it is of unvarying quality, but before 'voiced' consonants and in open syllables the tongue rises to a closer position, as in *food* and *two*.

When any of these vowels is immediately followed by another vowel in slow, formal speech the back closing is followed or realized by a slight [w] glide:

queueing	/kjuɪŋ/	[kjuʷɪŋ]
bowing	/baʊɪŋ/	[baʷɪŋ]
snowing	/snəʊɪŋ/	[snəʷɪŋ]
doing	/duɪŋ/	[duʷɪŋ]

Most of the words containing the vowels in column D have an *r* in the spelling which is of course pronounced in 'r'-pronouncing accents of English. When the *r* occurs in the spelling immediately before a vowel the *r* is pronounced in RP. The following examples show:

(a) words which have a final *r*
(b) the final *r* being followed by a vowel
(c) examples of words which are pronounced with the relevant vowel in RP but which have no *r* in the spelling:

	1	2	3
/ɪə/	hear	hearing	idea
/eə/	air	airing	—
/ɑ/	tar	tarring	calm, path, ah, laugh
/ɔ/	core	coring	caught, law, talk
/ʊə/	tour	touring	fluent
/ɜ/	purr	purring	colonel

/eə/ begins with the front of the tongue in half-open position. The front is depressed as the centre of the tongue rises to just about half-open position. The prominence is on the first element of this diphthong. There is a strong tendency, especially among younger speakers, for this vowel to be realized as a long, half-open front vowel, especially before 'voiced' consonants and in word final position as in *cared, bear,* /eə/ thus follows the pattern already established by the simplification of /ar/ and /or/, through /aə/ and /ɔə/, to /ɑ/ and /ɔ/. So /er/ to /eə/ yields [ɛː].

/ɔ/ is realized as a half-open, back vowel with considerable protrusion of the corners of the mouth and pouting of the lips. It is a type of rounding that shows the inner side of the lips, rather than the type involving tight closure of the lips round a tiny central space as for /u/. It is a very long vowel. Some speakers, especially in the London area, realize this with slight diphthongization as [ɔə]. For those who have difficulty in distinguishing /ɒ/ and /ɔ/ the simplest distinction may be made in terms of the very much more marked *pouting* rounding for /ɔ/ and its much greater length.

/ʊə/ begins with the back of the tongue in half-close position, then this lowers as the centre rises to between half-open and half-close. This phoneme is rapidly disappearing in the speech of younger RP speakers as it merges with /ɔ/. For such speakers the examples given above would be realized as /tɔ/ and /flɔnt/ respectively. Even though for many such speakers some isolated lexical items appear to retain /ʊə/—*moor* is such a one—these items remain as fossilized forms—/ʊə/ for all practical purposes does not exist as a phoneme in the speech of many younger RP speakers.

When any vowels in this column are followed immediately by a vowel in a second syllable, the two vowels are normally separated by an [r] glide when there is an *r* in the spelling:

hearing	/hɪərɪŋ/	[hɪˀrɪŋ]
airing	/eərɪŋ/	[eˀrɪŋ]
tarring	/tɑrɪŋ/	[tɑrɪŋ]
coring	/kɔrɪŋ/	[kɔrɪŋ]
touring	/tʊərɪŋ/	[tʊrɪŋ] or /tɔərɪŋ/ [tɔrɪŋ]
purring	/pɜrɪŋ/	[pɜrɪŋ]

When there is no *r* in the spelling, the speaker has a choice:

(a) pronouncing the liasion as though there were an *r* in the spelling, yielding *idea of* [aɪdɪˀrɒv], *law and order* [lɔrənɔdə]

(b) interrupting the vowel sequence with a glottal stop: [aɪdɪəˀɒv], [lɔˀənɔdə]

(c) introducing a [w] glide if the vowel concerned has strong lip rounding: [lɔwənɔdə]

(d) allowing the two vowels to coalesce into one vowel: [lɔːnɔdə].

Some speakers make use of this last option even when there is an *r* in the spelling, so one may hear *far away* realized as [fɑːweɪ].

2.3.1 The transcription of vowels

There are many different transcriptions of English available (cf. Abercrombie, 1964a). I have preferred not to use the most widely known, that of Daniel Jones' *English Pronouncing Dictionary*, because I have found the use of the length symbol for the vowels especially in pairs like /iː/. /i/; /uː/, /u/ misleading for many foreign students. They tend to interpret the length symbol as indicating length wherever it occurs, even before 'voiceless' consonants. This means that the essential contrast of vowel length before 'voiceless' and 'voiced' consonants is obscured. I have used instead a slightly modified version of the transcription used in *A Dictionary of Contemporary English* (1978) (see Table 1 on page 21). This avoids the use of the length mark and introduces as few exotic symbols as is practicable.

2.4 The 'ideal' syllable and the 'ideal' word

One of the most striking differences between slow colloquial pronunciation and informal speech lies in the way the structure of syllables and words is simplified and altered in informal speech. In this section we shall, very briefly, discuss some of the constraints on the structure of syllables and words in slow colloquial pronunciation. In Chapter 4 we shall see how these constraints may be modified in informal speech.

There are constraints on the sequences of consonants which can occur initially in monosyllabic words. We shall state some of the more obvious constraints* here (see Table 1, p. 21):

(a) no member of any column may cluster with its own approximant—so we may find *twist, dwell, quick, swift, thwack* but not *tl-, *dl-, *θl-; *pray, bray, fray, tray, drown, throw, shriek, crow, grow* but not *sr-.

(b) no member of column D may cluster except /ʃ/ with /r/ as in *shriek*.

(c) /m/ and /n/ may only cluster with /s/ as in *smear* and *sneer*. /ŋ/ does not occur initially.

(d) /s/ may precede any member of row 1 except /tʃ/— see point (b); all members of row 4 except /j/†—see point (b)—and /r/ see point (a); /m/ and /n/—see point (c); and /f/ in rare Greek borrowings like *sphere*.

(e) all three term clusters must begin with /s/, have a 'voiceless' stop as the second member (i.e. /p, t, k/) and an approximant (as allowed by point (a) above) as third member, for example *split, straight, squirt.*

Many other constraints on the structure of monosyllables could be stated.

If we examine the structures of polysyllabic words we will find that it is possible to analyse any sequence of consonants which we find medially in a word into two parts, the first of which may occur as the final cluster in a monosyllabic word and the second of which may occur as the initial cluster in a monosyllabic word. However, if we listen carefully to how English speakers divide up words we may find that they produce phonetic forms which do not conform to the regularity I have just stated. We may find words divided up phonetically in ways which our analysis does not allow: e.g. *meadow* with the division /me/ + /dəʊ/, *butler* with the division /bʌ/ + /tlə/, *pixie* with the division /pɪ/ + /ksɪ/. In all of these examples the first syl-

---

* For a full description of phonotactic possibilities, see Gimson (2nd edition, 1970, paragraph 9.08).

† Note that in this analysis the sequence /sju/ as in *pseudonym* is analysed as consonant /s/ plus vowel /ju/.

lable contains one of the 'basic' vowel series which, it is usually claimed, can only occur in a syllable closed by a consonant. In the second and third examples the second syllable begins with the sequences /tl/ and /ks/ respectively, sequences which are excluded by the regularities we have stated. In order not to be confused by the apparent conflict between some of the data that we may observe and some of the regularities that we have stated we need to make it very clear that there are two different levels of statement here. The statement of the regularities governing the structure of monosyllabic and polysyllabic words in English is made at an *idealized, phonological* level. It is a statement of the same sort of level as the one where we listed the phonemes of English. It asserts that there will not be introduced into English, words which have initial clusters like tl-, pt-, ml-, or final clusters like -lzg, -bdg, -kfð, or medial sequences like -mrsg-, -sʃsʃ-, -pbw-. The syllable at this level of description is conceived of as the *unit of distribution* of phonemes. We might coin the term 'distributional syllable' for it.

We need however to be able to appeal to a notion of syllable when we are describing phonetic performance. I shall call the syllable at this level of description the 'phonetic syllable'. We can say then that the word *butler* which can be analysed into the distributional syllables /bʌt/ + /lə/ may be realized by a speaker by the sequence of phonetic syllables /bʌ/ + /tlə/. It may of course also be realized by some speakers, or indeed the same speaker on another occasion, as the sequence of phonetic syllables /bʌt/ + /lə/ where the phonetic syllables are in a very direct relationship with the distributional syllables. In Chapter 4 we will encounter many examples of data where the phonetic syllable differs markedly from the distributional syllable. Even in slow formal speech we will find that individuals differ in the way they divide up the phonetic syllables of polysyllabic words. Consider the word *extraordinary*. In very explicit speech it may have six syllables divided like this: /ek/ + /strə/ + /ɔ/ + /dɪ/ + /nə/ + /rɪ/. (There may well be some local disagreement about how these phonetic syllable boundaries are assigned—I simply spoke the word as I might over a noisy telephone wire and found that, on this occasion, this is how I divided it.) But very commonly, and still in formal speech it may be pronounced with five phonetic syllables—/ɪk/ + /strɔ/ + /dɪ/ + /nə/ + /rɪ/—or even four—/ɪk/ + /strɔ/ + /dɪn/ + /rɪ/. We know very little about the principles by which people divide words into phonetic syllables. Many individuals seem to prefer to divide words into a sequence of phonetic syllables which are not closed by a consonant, yielding a preferred structure consonant-vowel + consonant-vowel + consonant-vowel—as in my pronunciation of *extraordinary* discussed above. Where this preference would give rise to phonetic consonant sequences which are prohibited within the distributional syllable, most speakers seem to prefer a solution which yields a sequence in the phonetic syllable which is allowed in the distributional syllable. Thus *spanking* will tend to be realized as /spæŋ/ + /kɪŋ/ rather than as /spæ/ + /ŋkɪŋ/, *dumpling* as /dʌm/ + /plɪŋ/ rather than as /dʌ/ + /mplɪŋ/ and *acted* as /æk/ + /tɪd/ rather than as /æ/ + /ktɪd/. However, as we have already observed in discussing possible realizations of *butler* and *pixie*, some speakers will produce phonetic syllables which do not conform to the constraints stated for the distributional syllables. It seems probable that, at the phonetic level, some syllable initial sequences which are prohibited at the distributional level are less likely than others. It is quite usual to find initial sequences of /t/ or /d/ + /l/, and 'voiceless' stops followed by /s/ as in *extra*—/e/ + /kstrə/.

People sometimes suggest that wherever possible they will make the phonetic syllable break coincide with a morpheme boundary. This suggestion seems very plausible in words like *football, ice-cream* and *mousetrap.* However, the tendency to produce phonetic syllables of a consonant-vowel structure may be more important than the morpheme boundary in forms like *nosey* and *worthless* which are likely to be realized phonetically as /nəʊ/ + /zɪ/ and /wɜ/ + /θləs/. I think the influence of morpheme boundaries in determining phonetic syllabification is very weak compared with that of the preference for consonant-vowel structured syllables. One might also point to the common usage in the furniture trade of referring to *wardrobes* as *drobes.*

Let us briefly summarize the main points made in this section:

(a) The distributional syllable conforms to very strict constraints on consonant and vowel sequences.

(b) Any sequence of consonants within a polysyllabic word must be capable of being divided in such a way that some of the consonants can be assigned to an acceptable distributional syllable final cluster and the rest can be assigned to an acceptable distributional syllable initial cluster.

(c) Constraints on phonetic syllables are less stringent than those that operate at the distributional level. (Further discussion of this point may be found in 4.2.)

3 The function of rhythm

3.1 The rhythmic structure of English

Every language has its own characteristic rhythm and one of the most difficult areas to master of the spoken form of a foreign language is that of rhythm. The rhythm is part of the general *look* of how the speakers of their language speak it. It is intimately bound in with the whole muscular setting which characterizes the speakers of different languages—the way the head is held and moved during speech, the way the lower jaw and tongue are held in relation to the upper jaw, the great variety of bodily movement of different kinds which help us to identify speakers of different languages even without hearing them speak. It takes a great deal of confidence to be able to put aside the identifying muscular characteristics of one's own language and adopt those of another, and very few teaching programmes will find time to try to teach students to master anything so difficult. It is however essential that students should be encouraged to be aware of these characteristics. This is because rhythm in English is not just something extra, added to the basic sequence of consonants and vowels, it is the guide to the structure of information in the spoken message.

We will begin by discussing what rhythm *is* and then go on to discuss its function. The rhythm of English is based on the contrast of stressed and unstressed syllables. If you watch an English speaker talking you will be able to see, without hearing what he is saying, where the stressed syllables are. All the big muscular movements that he makes are in time with the stressed syllables. When he waves his arms, nods his head, puts his foot down, raises his eyebrows, frowns, opens his jaw more widely, purses his lips; all this is done in time with the rhythm of speech. This is of course hardly surprising. All human physical activity which is extended in time tends to be rhythmical activity—breathing, running, walking, sewing, knitting, swimming, peeling potatoes for example. The rhythm may not be absolute, some 'strokes' may be missing and some may be mistimed but there is a sense in which all these activities can get into 'a rhythmical swing'. Speech is just like these other activities. There is a tendency for a rhythm to be established in speech. The rhythmic beat in English is the stressed syllable. These beats will coincide with other muscular beats of the body. This unity of bodily rhythm and speech rhythm is particularly clearly seen in the case of the stutterer who, when he gets stuck on an articulation, may enlarge some other muscular rhythm—nod his head or tap with his foot—in trying to re-establish the speech rhythm.

The stressed syllables and their accompanying muscular movements elsewhere in the body will tend to occur at roughly equal intervals of time but just as in other human activities, swimming for instance, some beats will be slightly early, some slightly late and some may be missing altogether. The more organized the speech the more rhythmical it will be. Thus, in general, prose read aloud by a fluent reader has a much more obvious rhythm than conversational speech which may be full of pauses and false starts. Very fluent speakers, who can organize their thoughts well in advance of actually uttering them, also establish a far more obvious rhythm than those who have to search for the right word and keep trying to refine a thought while in the middle of expressing it. So we can say that there is a tendency to establish a rhythm. The rhythmic beat will consist of stressed syllables. Any unstressed syllables occurring between the stressed syllables will be compressed as far as possible in order to allow the next stressed syllable to come on the regular beat. In the following example each stressed syllable is underlined:

The elec<u>tri</u>city <u>board</u> <u>stat</u>ed that they would be o<u>bli</u>ged to con<u>si</u>der the <u>re</u>intro<u>du</u>ction of <u>pow</u>er <u>cuts</u>.

This example was read in the manner shown here by a radio news reader. Now it is quite clear that the stressed syllables are not divided by an equal number of unstressed syllables. We can show this by representing the stressed syllables by capital *A*s and the unstressed syllables by small *a*s:

ɑɑɑAɑɑAAɑɑɑɑɑɑAɑɑAɑɑAɑɑAɑɑAɑA

You will notice that there is a fairly strong *Aaa* pattern in this sentence. All the examples of *Aaa* can be expected to be of pretty much the same length, so the sequences

<u>tri</u>city
<u>bli</u>ged to con
<u>si</u>der the
<u>re</u>intro
<u>duc</u>tion of

set a strong rhythmic pattern in this sentence. What happens then when there is a sequence of two stressed syllables, of *AA* as in <u>board</u> <u>sta</u>(ted)? The answer is that the first of the *A* syllables will be stretched in time, not, certainly, so that it takes up as much time as *Aaa* but, still, it is longer than it would have been if it had been immediately followed by an unstressed syllable. What happens to the sequence of six *a* syllables is even more dramatic—they are squashed closely together in time so that they are heard as an acoustic blur rather than a series of six separate syllables. We shall talk more about what happens to such syllables in the next chapter. The point to notice here is the following. Any speaker (or any writer if we are considering reading aloud) will set up a dominant rhythmic *foot*. In the sentence above, and indeed throughout the whole of the news broadcast that this sentence was abstracted from, the dominant foot was of the pattern *Aaa*,—stress, unstress, unstress. The beat comes on the *A* and then there is a space for the *aa*. However not every foot will be of this structure—some feet, as we have seen, may be of the structure *A*, some of the structure *Aaaaaaa*. Any deviation from the *Aaa* foot structure will throw the beat off for a moment but then it will briefly re-emerge, be lost again, re-emerge and so on. You may wonder why I choose to state the foot pattern as *Aaa* rather than *aAa* or *aaA*. The reason is that if we have a sequence like <u>tri</u>city <u>board</u> <u>sta</u>ted it is <u>board</u> that gets stretched in time, not <u>sta</u>(ted). (For a discussion of the foot structure of English see Abercrombie, 1964b).

3.1.1 Stressed and unstressed syllables

The face of the speaker will always give a visual clue to the stressed syllables. Even an impassive speaker who has very few obvious extraneous movements while he is speaking will make larger gestures with his jaw and lips in producing the initial consonants and the vowels of stressed syllables than in producing unstressed syllables.

Stressed syllables are sometimes said to be produced with more 'force' than unstressed syllables. Experiments have shown that there is no single variable which is always present in stressed syllables and is not present in unstressed syllables. 'Force' must be interpreted in a very general way. Some syllables which are perceived as stressed are louder than the surrounding unstressed syllables but sometimes there is no measurable difference of loudness. Some stressed syllables are spoken on a higher pitch than surrounding unstressed syllables—but a sudden dramatic drop in pitch may have the effect of marking a stressed syllable. Any syllable on which the pitch of the voice moves perceptibly—whether the pitch rises or falls—will be perceived as stressed. Any syllable which is markedly longer than the surrounding syllables will also be perceived as stressed. (From the point of view of teaching production of stress, *length* is the variable that most students find easiest to control, and is a reliable marker of stress. Speakers of languages where each syllable is roughly equal in length would do well to practise producing English stressed syllables with a count of two on each stress as against one on unstressed syllables.)

One valuable guide to learning to distinguish stressed from unstressed syllables is the degree of explicitness of articulation of the syllable. In a stressed syllable the initial consonant(s) and the vowel will be comparatively clearly enunciated whereas in an unstressed syllable the consonants may be very weakly enunciated and the vowel very obscure. It is important to realize that this is a feature of slow colloquial speech just as much as it is of informal speech. This is another area in which the dilemma of the teacher who is teaching foreign students to speak English is particularly apparent. On the one hand he knows quite well that there are unstressed syllables in English—every text book writes about them and every pronouncing dictionary marks the stressed syllable and leaves the unstressed syllables unmarked. On the other hand he is anxious to offer the most explicitly pronounced model for his students to copy. This frequently results in very little distinction being made between the pronunciation of stressed and unstressed syllables in the model that the students are offered. The unstressed syllables in such models are just as clearly pronounced as the stressed syllables—the only difference between them lies in pitch, loudness and length. This is a particularly unfortunate model since it is a model of spoken English which is never spoken *to* native English speakers *by* native English speakers. It is spoken exclusively to foreigners. The trouble is not simply that it is not a model of natural English, but that it accustoms students to listen for a set of segmental clues which will be denied them when they come to listen to English native speakers speaking naturally. Constant exposure to this sort of 'spoken English' means that students find it quite impossible to understand normal spoken English. They do not learn to rely on the structural information given them by the rhythm of speech but rely instead upon clear and distinct pronunciation of all vowels and consonants.

In slow colloquial English, just as much as in informal English, the consonants and vowels of unstressed syllables are less explicitly pronounced than those of stressed syllables. Unfortunately this is a 'more or less' statement. It is impossible to say that *all* unstressed syllables will lose such and such a characteristic which a stressed syllable will not lose. We are again talking in terms of tendencies. All things being equal, the following tendencies will be observed:

(a) Stops which are initial in stressed syllables will be pronounced with a moment of firm closure which completely obstructs the airstream. 'Voiceless' stops will be followed by aspiration. Stops initial in an unstressed syllable will be weakly articulated— it may be that the closure will not be completely closed, resulting either in a very weak stop or a slightly fricative-sounding stop. Thus for the second stop in each of the words *paper, baby,* the lips may not form a complete closure; the gesture of closure is not completed.

(b) Fricatives initial in a stressed syllable will have more friction and last longer than those initial in an unstressed syllable. For example the initial /s/ in *ceasing* will be more fricative and longer than the second.

(c) Vowels in stressed syllables will have the qualities associated with them as they were described in Chapter 2, for instance 'round' vowels will have lip rounding and diphthongs will be diphthongized. The 'same' vowels in unstressed syllables will be more obscure in quality, 'round' vowels will not have lip rounding and diphthongs will not be diphthongized. For example, when /ɪə/ in *here* is in stressed position, as in *come here,* the quality of the diphthong is clearly heard, but in unstressed position as in *he comes here constantly,* the /ɪə/ is pronounced as a sort of very obscure /e/.

It should be clear from this description that it is not sufficient simply to describe unstressed syllables in terms of the shwa vowel /ə/ and the 'reduced' vowel [ɪ] as is sometimes done. Not all unstressed vowels are reduced to these vowels, as we have just seen in our example, and the reduction in explicitness of pronunciation of the consonants is just as marked as the reduction of the vowel quality.

In general, stressed syllables will be marked by standing out in pitch against the surrounding unstressed syllables—either by the pitch moving, or being higher or lower than the surrounding unstressed syllables, by being longer and louder than unstressed syllables and by being pronounced more distinctly. Notice that I have not attempted to distinguish three or four 'degrees' of stress. At the moment I only wish to draw the distinction between unstressed syllables and all syllables which are at all stressed. I do not wish to imply by this that all stressed syllables in an utterance are perceived as equally prominent. On the contrary, stressed syllables that are produced with moving pitch or high pitch will be perceived as more prominent in general than stressed syllables produced on mid or low pitch. I shall attribute this variation in perceived prominence to the effect of the intonation of the utterance in which the syllables occur.

3.1.2 Pause: 'rests' in rhythm

So far I have spoken of rhythm in English speech as the alternation of stressed and unstressed syllables. We need now to add to this account the way in which pauses contribute to the structure of the rhythm, just as rests in music participate in the rhythm of music. A frequent way of pronouncing *thank you* in everyday English is to say [kːjʊ], where there is a nod of the head on the long consonant [kː] and then as the head moves up, out of the nod, the remaining unstressed syllable [kjʊ] is uttered. The stressed syllable *thank* is not actually uttered but seems to be reflected by the muscular movement which produces the downward movement of the nod, while the unstressed syllable is uttered on the upbeat. This is an instance where a brief pause replaces a stressed syllable in the stream of speech. If you stand by the cash desk in a canteen or by the checkout point in a British supermarket, you will observe innumerable examples of this phenomenon.

More obvious examples of pause occur regularly in speech which is read aloud from a punctuated text: the reader-aloud will leave short pauses at commas, longer pauses at full stops (and question marks and exclamation marks), and even longer pauses at the boundaries of paragraphs. These pauses are integrated by a competent reader into the overall rhythmic structure of speech and contribute to our perception of a fluent, rhythmical flow of language. Pauses occur on the rhythmic beat, just as stressed syllables do. A short pause, for a comma, will contribute a single beat, whereas longer pauses contribute multiple beats. (Again the analogy may be drawn with rests in music which may be of different durations but must enter into the established units of rhythm in the piece.)

The part played by pause in the establishment of rhythm in speech is particularly clearly manifested in certain sorts of rhythmically regular verse, perhaps most clearly of all in nursery rhymes—remember that the crucial feature of a nursery rhyme is that you establish a regular beat as you sway your baby back and forth in your arms. (A further use for them is as skipping rhymes where the beat coincides with each dip of the hand as the rope is twirled and, again, the regularity of the beat is essential.) Consider the first lines of 'Three Blind Mice' from this point of view. The most characteristic rendering appears to be:

Three	blind	mice	
A	A	A	A
Three	blind	mice	
A	A	A	A
See	how they	run	
A	A	A	A
See	how they	run	
A	A	A	A

where each A represents a beat, and there is a silent beat at the end of each line. In such a rendering the four beats in each of the first lines carry on in the rest of the rhyme, so all lines contain four beats.

They all run	after the	farmer's	wife
A	A	A	A
who cut off their	tails with a	carving	knife
A	A	A	A
did ever you see such a	thing in your	life	
A	A	A	A
as three	blind	mice	
A	A	A	A

You will notice that in this latter part of the rhyme, unstressed syllables appear at the beginning of each line. How do these fit into the pattern? They are the weak syllables of the last stressed beat in the preceding line—they are examples of what is traditionally called 'enjambment'—the running on of one line into the next, which in this rhyme mimics the scurrying of the mice. The foot structure can be laid out in the following way:

Three	all run
blind	after the
mice	farmer's
A	wife Who
Three	cut off their
blind	tails with a
mice	carving
A	knife Did
See	ever you
how they	see such a
run	thing in your
A	life As
See	three
how they	blind
run	mice
A They	A

It will be clear that a series of monosyllables in a verse line will have the effect of slowing down the speech as each of these syllables takes up a longer space, as in 'Three Blind Mice', whereas a series of feet containing several unstressed syllables will appear faster, as the syllables are crammed together within a foot.

The rhythmic structure of prose is naturally a good deal less regular than that of verse; nonetheless, a competent reader-aloud will read in such a way as to set up a pattern of expectation. Fluent public speakers who are speaking spontaneously will often also produce a rhythmic structure whose pattern recurs sufficiently often to give an overall rhythmical effect. This is particularly the case when what is said has already been rehearsed on previous occasions. The rhythmic structure of conversation, however, is generally much less obvious and, particularly where a speaker is working out a concept for the first time and finding it hard to express, the resulting speech may be dense in pauses, so much so that it may appear disfluent, and hence may be hard to understand. This is because the main function of pauses is to indicate to the listener which chunks of language need to be co-interpreted, interpreted as a single chunk, and which chunks are to be separated off—the longer the pause, the further the separation: thus a 'comma' pause usually identifies the edges of phrases, a 'full-stop' pause the edges of sentences, and a 'paragraph' pause the boundaries of larger chunks of discourse. As I have suggested by talking of the pauses in these terms, they function in speech very much as punctuation functions in written language—to indicate to the person being addressed the intended structure of the utterance. (See 5.3 extracts 1–4 for examples of this.)

3.2 The function of stress

3.2.1 Word stress

The contrast of stress and unstress has two distinct functions in English. We shall consider the best known function first. All words have stress patterns which are quite stable when the word is pronounced in isolation. The stress pattern of a polysyllabic word is a very important identifying feature of the word. It must not be regarded as an adjunct to a correctly pronounced sequence of consonants and vowels but as the essential framework within which the consonants and vowels are related. There is a certain amount of evidence that native speakers rely very strongly on the stress pattern of a word in order to identify it. It is suggested that we 'store' words under stress patterns, so if a word of a given stress pattern is pronounced, in processing this word we bring to bear our knowledge of that part of the vocabulary which bears this pattern. And we find it difficult to interpret an utterance in which a word is pronounced with the wrong stress pattern—we begin to 'look up' possible words under this wrong stress pattern. I remember a student asking me a question about /əˈnimɪzm/ in *King Lear* which I was unable to understand at first. I assumed that he must meant something to do with *anaemia* which has, of course, an appropriate stress pattern for the form that he produced. Eventually I arrived at /ˈænimɪzm/. Notice that although *animism* makes sense in the context whereas *anaemia* does not, my instantly preferred interpretation was one that held the stress pattern that had been produced, even though this involved supposing that both segmental and semantic errors had been made.

Other evidence that one of the ways we have of classifying words is in terms of their stress patterns comes from research done on the types of errors which are found when 'slips of the tongue' occur. These are a good deal more frequent in ordinary speech than might be supposed, and particularly so when the speaker is tired. The most common type of tongue slip involves the interaction of the stressed syllables of two words of the same stress pattern, as in 'I dropped a sholling in my shipping basket' (quoted by Boomer and Laver, 1968).

Another frequent class of errors involves the substitution of words of the same syllable structure which are semantically closely related, as in:

I'll try to provide a question—answer—as soon as possible.
He'll have to rent—let—his flat.
That's quite wrong—I mean right.

The substitution of words of the same stress and syllable pattern is well observed by Sheridan in the character of Mrs Malaprop in *The Rivals*:

. . . to *illiterate* him from your memory (eliminate)
. . . few gentleman nowadays know how to value the
    ineffectual qualities in a woman (intellectual)
. . . she should have a *supercilious* knowledge in accounting
    (superficial)

It seems probable that the identification of words by stress patterns is a process which characterizes the learning of English by young children who are native speakers of English. It seems always to be the case that the toddler who is beginning to learn to talk produces the stressed syllable of a word though some of the unstressed syllables may be ignored. So a common way of pronouncing *banana* is ['nanə], or *tomato* is ['matə] where in each case the initial unstressed syllable is not pronounced, and indeed there will be many examples of even more of the word being lost while the stressed syllable is preserved as in [luːli] for *usually*. It is hardly surprising, then, that the stressed syllable of a word is crucial to its identification.

There is some variability in stress patterns of particular classes of words in different accents of English. This variability does not affect the main stressed syllable of a word but affects the way syllables which would be unstressed in RP are pronounced. Many Scottish accents, for instance, produce unstressed syllables where the vowel quality is much more distinct than it is in RP and with noticeably longer unstressed vowels. This, combined with stressed vowels which are a good deal shorter than they are in RP, yields a characteristically different rhythmic impression, much more like a 'syllable timed' language than RP. The class of polysyllabic words beginning with unstressed *con*, as in *condition*, *confusion* or *conceal*, is pronounced with a full vowel in the first syllable /kɔn/, in a number of Midlands accents and in Yorkshire, though the stressed syllable is still the perceptually most prominent syllable.

3.2.2 Stressed words in sentences

Whereas every word which is pronounced in isolation must bear a stress, when words are combined in utterances not all words are stressed. Thus for example pronouns like *he* and *who* must be stressed when they are pronounced in isolation but when they are pronounced in sentences they are rarely stressed. In the sentences *he called on the prime minister* and *the man who was found in the Shankill Road area was already dead,* *he* and *who* will be unstressed except in the rare case when they are contradicting some previous remark as in *He—not she—called on the prime minister.* We shall leave such contradictory, 'contrastive' stress until the chapter on intonation. In all cases where 'contrastive stress' is not involved, nearly all *grammatical words* will lose their stress when they are combined together to form an utterance, whereas nearly all *lexical words* will keep their stress. Grammatical words are the words that show the relations between the parts of an utterance—conjunctions, prepositions, pronouns and so on. Lexical words are the words that carry the meaning of the utterance—nouns, main verbs, adjectives and adverbs. The function of stress then is to mark the meaning words, the information-bearing words in the utterance. Consider the following sentences:

1 The discharged prisoners' aid society will be organizing a number of demonstrations.
2 The meeting of the two prime ministers has had to be postponed.
3 Areas in the west of Scotland escaped their expected electricity cut this morning.

There is no one way of reading these sentences—by stressing different words the 'same' sentences are interpreted rather differently. There are however a number of words in each sentence which will have to be stressed no matter how the sentence is interpreted. In 1 *discharged, prisoners, aid, society, organizing, demonstrations;* in 2 *meeting, prime ministers, postponed;* in 3 *areas, west, Scotland, escaped, electricity cut,* will have to be stressed in any reading. In each case what is being talked about, the subject of the sentence, and what is being said about the subject, must be stressed. There are other words which might be stressed in a deliberate slow colloquial style—in 1 *number;* in 2 *two;* in 3 *expected, morning.* In each case we see that it is a modifier which may be stressed in a slow colloquial rendering but may be unstressed in a more rapid rendering. Apart from these modifiers there is no choice—the lexical words already mentioned *must* be stressed and the grammatical words *must* be unstressed. (Bear in mind that we are not here considering the possibility of 'contrastive' stress—the sentences we are considering are spoken out of context.)

A quick indication of the essential words in a message can be given by considering which words would have to be included in a telegram or a newspaper headline. Possible headlines for our three sentences might be: 1 DISCHARGED PRISONERS AID SOCIETY ORGANIZING DEMONSTRATIONS, 2 PRIME MINISTERS' MEETING POSTPONED, and 3 WEST SCOTLAND AREAS ESCAPE ELECTRICITY CUT. It may be objected that we have no way of knowing that the native speaker relies especially on hearing the stressed words in an utterance in order to be able to interpret it. We have however a very significant window on the behaviour of native speakers in this respect in the behaviour of young children. It is well known that children who are just learning to speak produce utterances which are largely composed of nouns, verbs and adjectives: *Johnny all gone, silly pussy, daddy come,* all stressed words spoken with their individual correct stress patterns. It may also be observed that when very young children mimic something which has just been said to them they omit the unstressed grammatical words but repeat the lexical stressed words. So the utterance by the mother *come with Mummy* will be repeated by the child as *come Mummy, come Mummy.* Another indication of the native speaker's instinctive reliance on the importance of stressed words can be seen in the behaviour of someone speaking over a noisy telephone wire. A speaker who is finding difficulty in making himself heard does not shout separate and equally distinct syllables down the telephone. He shouts words or word groups, but words in their correct stress patterns with the stressed syllable especially loud and clear and the unstressed syllables just making enough noise and filling in enough time to show the frame in which the stressed syllables fit. Thus a sentence like *I won't be able to come on Monday* would be shouted down a noisy wire as:

I <u>won't</u>-be <u>able</u>-to <u>come</u>-on <u>Mon</u>day

The stressed syllables will be louder, longer, more prominent in pitch and very precisely articulated. The unstressed syllables will still be comparatively obscure.

It is widely agreed that unstress is a very difficult thing to teach. The difficulties arise for various reasons. In some languages each syllable is pronounced with the same amount of stress as all the other syllables and the notion of linguistic stress is completely alien—it just does not apply in such languages. The difficulty here is that a quite new linguistic concept has to be taught from scratch. For students who are accustomed to bundling consonants and vowels into success-ive syllables and pronouncing them all equally distinctly, equally loudly, and equally long, the sudden demand that they should com-bine some consonants and vowels into stressed syllables and some into unstressed syllables seems pointless and arbitrary. The difficulty is compounded by the fact that an unstressed syllable seems by its very nature to be an unsatisfactory, unfinished sort of object, some-how 'less correct' than a stressed syllable. For teachers who are accustomed always to ask a student for *more* of X and Y it is hard to have to start asking a student to produce *less,* especially when it is harder to hear whether the obscure form is correct than it was to hear that the explicit form was incorrect. It must be the heart-break-ing experience of many teachers that in trying to persuade a student to produce an acceptable form for *mother,* they work hard on the dental /ð/ and the shwa vowel /ə/. The student produces a careful and slow /ˈmʌ—ˈðə/. 'Good,' says the teacher, enthusiastically, 'Now let's get the stress pattern right: <u>Mo</u>ther.' The student now con-centrates on the stress pattern, and the carefully acquired /ð/ and /ə/ slip away as he produces a form that sounds to the teacher sus-piciously like /ˈmʌzʌ/. The teacher is now in a quandary. If he asks the student to repeat the form clearly enough for him to hear the consonant and vowel details of the second syllable, the stress pattern will certainly be lost. On the other hand he feels that having just been painstakingly establishing /ð/ and /ə/ he must not instantly allow the student to mispronounce them. It may be that in the early stages at least the teacher should try to concentrate stress pattern exercises on words which do not produce vowel and consonant dif-ficulties as well, but it is a hard task in a language which has such a complex set of vowels *and* /θ, ð/.

It may be that a more satisfactory approach to the teaching of the production of correct stress patterns may lie in the prior teaching of the *recognition* of stress patterns. Already many teachers use taped or recorded courses of stress exercises spoken by native speakers. (I have already mentioned the dangers of such courses when unstressed syl-lables are not properly unstressed.) Often students are required to mimic the patterns offered by these courses without having paused to consider just what it is that they are mimicking. Not surprisingly the exercise turns out to be fairly fruitless. It is well worth while carefully analysing, stressed syllable by stressed syllable, some sample patterns before the students begin the mimicking exercise. The aim here is to make the student *aware* of different ways of marking stress, and able to recognize stress and unstress rapidly and accurately enough to help him work out the structure of the message he is listening to.

It is this aspect of spoken English, more than any other, which the teacher of English to foreign students should concentrate on. From the point of view of production the correct pronunciation of /θ, ð/ and /ə/ fades into insignificance beside the ability to produce correct stress patterns on words. From the point of view of the comprehension of spoken English, the ability to identify stressed syllables and make intelligent guesses about the content of the message from this information, is absolutely essential.

4 Patterns of simplification in informal speech

Hitherto we have considered the forms of speech that we expect to hear spoken in a slow colloquial style of speech. We have described the 'ideal' consonants and vowels as they might occur in isolation, the 'ideal' syllable structure and the 'ideal' stress structure of words as they occur in this style. We noted in discussing the 'ideal' stress structure that even in a very slow, formal, style of speech the unstressed syllables are less explicitly pronounced than the stressed syllables.

In normal informal speech when the speaker is concentrating on what he is saying, and not on how he is saying it, he will tend to articulate in the most efficient manner—he will make articulatory gestures that are sufficient to allow the units of his message to be identified but he will reduce any articulatory gesture whose explicit movement is not necessary to the comprehension of his message. He will smooth out any articulatory gestures that he can do without—if his tongue is already in one position and the next consonant but one in a sequence requires the same tongue position, the intervening consonant may be smoothed out, if it is not initial in a stressed syllable. Thus in a sentence like *The spectators were crammed behind each other*, where there is a sequence /mdb/, there will be a very strong likelihood of the medial /d/ not being pronounced. In this chapter we are going to examine some of the regular patterns of simplification that occur in normal speech. Most of the examples cited were spoken by radio newsreaders or by academics, politicians or journalists speaking on the radio. They were all speakers who would be readily identified as RP speakers. They were all, obviously, speaking in a style which they felt was appropriate to the situation, a situation in which they were speaking to a large number of individuals who were not personally known to them and who were unable to see them. Most people (but not all) find it very much easier to understand what is being said when they can see the face of the speaker, his lip movements, his muscular movements indicating stress and his expression. Indeed one can often observe a change in the manner of speech of someone who gets up, while he is talking, and turns away from the person he was facing to look out of the window, answer the phone or the door. He speaks slightly more loudly and clearly as he turns away from the listener. So we may expect the style of speech we hear on the radio to be rather more explicit than the style of speech we encounter in face to face situations.

In attempting to describe the patterns of simplification in informal speech we are, in a sense, trying to do a ridiculous thing. We are putting under a magnifying glass some aspect of speech whose whole *raison d'être* is that it should not be consciously perceived. We are attempting to seize and examine a form which depends for its existence on the fact that it is obscure. If the speaker had had any notion that his pronunciation of a given form would have been the subject of discussion he certainly would not have pronounced it in this obscure way. As it is he spoke in a way which would allow his hearers to understand the message—making the meaningful elements of the message prominent and playing down the rest. In the context of the total message it is very unlikely that any native speaker would observe the details of the pronunciation. The native speaker would construct for himself an intelligible interpretation of what had been said—an interpretation which could always be referred to a very explicit form. For example, if he heard a form which we might transcribe as

/'stə'wɪlsn'wentə'daʊnɪŋstritət'wʌnts/

and was asked to repeat it slowly he would probably repeat it in the full, explicit, slow colloquial form:

/'mɪstə'wɪlsən'wenttə'daʊnɪŋstritət'wʌnts/

having understood the message as *Mr Wilson went to Downing Street at once.* There is no sense in which he can make a 'simplified' *interpretation* of the message. He must either make a total interpretation or none at all. (He might fail to understand a word in a structure whose form he has grasped and ask a question like 'Who was it went to Downing Street?', or 'Where was it that Mr Wilson went?', but one can hardly imagine a question, 'Was it a Mr or Mrs and what was the name and what did you say he or she did and where did he or she do it?'. If the listener has not found a structure to ask a question about, he will ask for a repetition of the whole utterance.) Unless the native speaker is the one-in-a-million person who is actually listening to *how* something is being said rather than to *what* is being said, the actual details of pronunciation will not impinge on him in a conscious way.

Indeed, in listening to normal speech it is important to realize that we do not perceive spoken language as a series of sounds which we then divide into words. As we saw in the last chapter we need at least to be able to identify the stressed syllable in a word, and its place in the word and the stressed words in the stream of speech. It is normally necessary to listen for several seconds to a radio broadcast or to a conversation that one has just joined in order to 'tune in' to what is being said. It is not possible simply to switch in automatically from the first segment you hear and then 'add' the following segments to your interpretation as they are uttered. It has been repeatedly shown in experiments that when listeners are played the first couple of segments of a word spliced out of the stream of speech, they are often unable even to recognize what the segments are. Even complete words are sometimes, in such conditions, literally unrecognizable—in one experiment over half the words heard could not be recognized and listeners could not determine which 'sounds' were being pronounced. And the listeners were educated adult native speakers of English. One reason for this phenomenon is that the phonetic cues to segments are not distributed in a simple linear way in the acoustic signal, as we pointed out at length in Chapter 2 in discussing where the cues for final 'voiced' consonants are located. A second reason is that in normal speech many of the cues which identify a word spoken in isolation are reduced or disappear altogether—this is the subject-matter of the rest of the current chapter. But perhaps the most important reason is that, in normal listening as native speakers of a language, we do not listen as if we were totally ignorant of the language, of what is being said, and of how that relates to our previous experience. We listen to the incoming signal actively predicting ends of words, ends of phrases, and sometimes whole chunks of expression. The phonetic cues we hear guide and check our interpretation but we are not solely reliant on them in arriving at it. In what follows, which describes some of the massive loss of phonetic detail in normal speech as opposed to words spoken slowly and clearly, it is important to remember that we are only partially reliant on the acoustic signal in forming an interpretation.

Clearly the situation is different for non-native speakers, listening to an unfamiliar language. For complex social and psychological reasons, they are less sure that they have grasped the topic being spoken of, the opinion being expressed about it, and the reasons for the speaker wanting to talk about it. They are less sure of the relevance of their own past experience in helping them to arrive at an interpretation. On top of all that, they are less sure of the forms of the language, the typical syntactic structures, and the conventional vocabulary to use in discussing this topic. For all these reasons foreign learners are less able to bring to bear 'top down' processing in forming an interpretation and, hence, are more reliant on 'bottom up' processing. If, in their education in the foreign language, they have in general been exposed to language spoken relatively slowly and clearly they are going to experience a devastating diminution of phonetic information at the segmental level when they encounter normal speech. Many of the cues which they are used to listening for will be denied them. We need then to be able to identify which are likely to disappear and which are the details which are likely to remain.

What we are going to try to do is to bring these details to our conscious notice. This, to begin with, is a very unnatural exercise. Further, we are going to abstract tiny details of segment sequences from a total message in which such details would not be at all obvious. We are going to ignore the obvious bits of the message and drag up the obscurities, the places which the speaker feels he can safely gloss over. Many of the forms which we examine might be condemned as 'vulgar' *if they occurred in stressed syllables in an utterance.* If any of my children produced such a form in a stressed syllable I should probably try to persuade the child to produce a more explicit form in that position. It is important to remember that the forms we examine would be unstressed, obscure, within the context of the total message. The only reason we are remarking on them is that we must prepare a student to do without a number of segmental clues in some parts of the utterance and we need to be able to show him what clues will go and what clues he can rely on finding.

I think it cannot be too strongly urged that students should not be required to *produce* the forms we examine here, only to recognize them and understand utterances in which they occur. Students are sometimes required to produce forms demonstrating 'assimilation' (which we shall discuss in 4.1). The difficulty with such exercises is that in order for the teacher to hear that the student is producing the required form the student has to make the form much too 'big', too obvious—as, indeed, the teacher had to do in demonstrating it. Refinements of pronunciation of this kind should be left for advanced students to adopt in appropriate circumstances by themselves. The teacher's aim here should be to make the student aware of the simplified forms so that he can understand them.

The difficulty faced by the student and teacher in producing forms out of context that sound much too 'big' is exactly the difficulty I face in presenting this chapter. Only by changing phonetic symbols or leaving a symbol out can I hope to show some variation in the pronunciation of a word, and very often I want to show something very much less gross, much less obvious than such a transcriptional variation would suggest. I shall therefore use diacritics with a meaning which I shall attempt to gloss in metaphoric terms in each case.

In quoting examples I shall enclose in square brackets the form that occurs in the data. Before each form in square brackets I shall give a slow colloquial form in phonemic slant brackets. The slow colloquial form represents a possible explicit pronunciation to which the informal form may be compared. Since in some cases there is more than one acceptable slow colloquial pronunciation of a form—as in the case of /ekə'nɒmɪks/ and /ikə'nɒmɪks/—and I have no way of knowing which form would have been chosen by the speaker if he had been uttering the word explicitly in isolation, I have had to make an arbitrary selection from the possible acceptable forms. It seems to me nonetheless that it is useful to have some sort of explicit form to compare the reduced form with. In general I have treated the whole phrase in slant brackets as a single unit—as it is treated in the data. This means that I have often given grammatical forms in their common reduced shape rather than in the shape they would have in isolation. I have written *to* in *to secure* as /təsɪ'kjuə/ rather than as /tusɪ'kjuə/. Where there are two common weak variants of a grammatical word when it occurs in context—as in the case of unstressed *been* which can be pronounced both as /bin/ and as /bɪn/—I have chosen to transcribe the less reduced form in the suggested slow colloquial pronunciation. In one section alone, 4.4, where I am discussing patterns of vowel reduction in unstressed syllables, I have represented the grammatical forms in the slow colloquial pronunciation as being in their most formal and explicit form. In this section I write /tusɪ'kjuə/ in the slant brackets so that the reduced form may be compared with the maximally explicit form.

The transcription in slant brackets should be interpreted as symbolizing what is known about slow colloquial pronunciation. Thus the transcription /tæp/ must be interpreted as implying, for instance, aspiration following the initial /t/ and a glottal stop preceding the final /p/. All the relevant standard information about the allophonic realization of vowels and consonants in different environments must be assumed to be implied by this transcription. The transcription in square brackets represents the particular speech act that we are interested in. Most of the symbols in the square brackets imply exactly what they imply when they appear in slant brackets. However where there is some difference between the slow colloquial form and the informal form I shall feel free to use symbols in the representation in square brackets which can not be used in a phonemic transcription since they do not symbolize English phonemes—the glottal stop symbol [ʔ] and and diacritics showing length [ː], nasalization [ɑ̃], and the realization of a consonant as a syllabic consonant [s̩].

4.1 Adjustment to surroundings

No segment occurs in the isolated state which we described in Chapter 2. Consonants and vowels are combined to form words and utterances within a rhythmic structure. Every consonant and every vowel will be affected by its neighbouring consonants and vowels and by the rhythmic structure in which it occurs. All vowels and most consonants are primarily articulated by movements of the tongue. We have only to consider the physical nature of the tongue—this bulky lump of muscle with a flexible tip—to see that if it gets into a given posture for one segment there will have to be a gradual undoing of that posture followed by a gradual assumption of another posture for the following segment. In fact segments follow each other so quickly that the tongue may not get into the 'ideal' position described in Chapter 2 at all. It will be pulled away by the preceding and following segments which themselves will be pulled away. This adjustment of each segment to its neighbours is a characteristic of all human speech. It is the main reason for the very wide variety of 'allophones' of each phoneme. The context, or environment, in which a phoneme occurs will determine the type of allophone which realizes the phoneme in that context. Different languages have different habits of adjustment—some prefer to adjust in one direction, some in another, some more, some less. Thus in all languages which allow a sequence of a phoneme /k/ and a phoneme /i/ the allophone of /k/ which occurs in the context of /i/ will be pronounced further forward on the palate than, say, the allophone of /k/ before a phoneme /u/. The allophone of English /k/ in *key* is pronounced with a closure of the middle of the tongue, between front and back, at about the point where the hard and soft palates join, whereas the allophone in *coo* is pronounced with the very back of the tongue making a closure with the back of the soft palate. In other languages the allophone of /k/ before /i/ may be much further forward on to the hard palate producing a sound not unlike that initial in English *cheese*, and the allophone before /u/ may be even further back than it is in English. The adaptation of segments to each other is then a universal fact of human language—the type of adaptation preferred will vary from one language to another.

This sort of inevitable adjustment is sometimes referred to as 'similitude' (Jones, 1962: 219; Abercrombie, 1967: 87). Each segment in every word that is pronounced, no matter how explicitly and clearly the word is pronounced, will be affected by this process of 'similitude'. When words are combined in the stream of speech their edges become available for the operation of this process. Since some deviation from the form of the word pronounced in isolation is involved here the process affecting the edges of words is referred to in the literature as 'assimilation' (Jones, 1962: 221; Abercrombie, 1967: 133). The phonetic details of the process may be identical—for example the forward posture of the tip of the tongue in the stop preceding the dental fricative in *width* may be identical to the posture for the stop before the dental fricative in *hid them*. However the forward adjustment will be present in all pronunciations of the word *width* whereas in isolation the final consonant of *hid* will not have this forward adjustment. We must add to this notion of assimilation at word boundaries the possibility of assimilation *within* a word when it is possible for there to be a pronunciation of a word in informal speech which is markedly different from that in the slow colloquial style—for example the slow colloquial pronunciation of *football* is /ˈfʊtbɔl/ but a very common informal pronunciation is [fʊʔpbɔl].

Let us now consider some examples of the assimilatory process which occur in my data:

1	/əˈmaʊntbaɪ/	[əˈmaʊmʔpbaɪ]	amount by
2	/ˈɡreɪtˈbrɪtən/	[ˈɡreɪʔpˈbrɪtən]	Great Britain
3	/ˈsteɪtmənt/	[ˈsteɪʔpmənt]	statement
4	/ˈθɜtɪˈfitˈwaɪd/	[ˈθɜtɪˈfiʔpˈwaɪd]	thirty feet wide
5	/ˈbændfəˈlaɪf/	[ˈbæmbfəˈlaɪf]	banned for life
6	/ˈhʌndrədˈpaʊndz/	[ˈhʌndrəbˈpaʊndz]	hundred pounds
7	/ˈvæŋɡɑdˈmuvmənt/	[ˈvæŋɡɑbˈmuvmənt]	vanguard movement
8	/ˈkɒmənwelθ/	[ˈkɒməmwelθ]	Commonwealth
9	/ˈwaʊntˈɡəʊ/	[ˈwaʊŋʔkˈɡəʊ]	won't go
10	/ˈɑmədˈkɑ/	[ˈɑməɡˈkɑ]	armoured car
11	/ˈmeksɪkənˈɡeɪmz/	[ˈmeksɪkəŋˈɡeɪmz]	Mexican games
12	/bɪnˈkɒnsəntreɪtɪŋ/	[ˈbɪŋˈkɒnsəntreɪtɪŋ]	been concentrating

13 /ˈðɪsjɪə/   [ˈðɪʃjɪə]   this year
14 /ˈtaɪmzˈʃeə/   [ˈtaɪmʒˈʃeə]   (Financial)
                                          Times Share
                                          (Index)
15 /kʌmfrəm/   [kʌɱfrəm]   come from
16 /aɪmˈɡəʊɪŋ/   [aɪŋˈɡɜŋ]   I'm going

The first point I would like to make about these examples is that they are quite typical of the sort of examples that you would find if you listened carefully to the first five minutes of any news broadcast. They are not rare types which you would be lucky to hear. Hardly a sentence passes without at least one such example occurring and with some speakers the assimilatory process occurs whenever the appropriate circumstances come together in the stream of speech.

In order for this sort of assimilation to occur it is necessary to have a syllable or word final consonant drawn from the group /t, d, n, m, s, z/ and, immediately following this, a word or syllable initial consonant that is either a velar or a labial consonant. All the examples except the last involve a sequence of consonants within a major constituent of the sentence, a noun phrase or a verb phrase.

The great majority of assimilations involve /t, d/ and /n/ exemplified in numbers 1–12 of the examples here. The other types are comparatively rare. It is important to realize that what is involved in an assimilation is not simply the replacement of the phoneme that occurs in slow colloquial speech by another phoneme. The transcription is misleading in this respect. In examples 1–3, which involve sequences /t/ + /b/ and /t/ + /m/, no closure for the /t/ is heard in the informal realization. There is however a very marked glottal stop before the stop—more like the strong glottal stop associated with final /t/ in for example *peat* than that associated with final /p/ in *peep*. It is the timing of the onset of lip closure that suggests the transcription [mˀpbaɪ], [ˀpb] and [ˀpm]. Notice that in example 1 this lip closure extends over the nasal preceding the final stop as well as the stop itself. In cases where final /t, d, n/ and a velar consonant are involved the transcription is again misleading. It suggests that the velar stop is untouched by the assimilatory process affecting the preceding consonant. It is true that the velar stop in each case remains identifiably velar but the stop is pulled forward on to the palate rather as it is in the articulation of /k/ in *key*. So in examples 9–12 not only are the members of the /t, d, n/ set pulled back along the roof of the mouth but also the velar stop is pulled forward. The same interaction can be observed in examples 13 and 14 where in

each case /s/ and /z/ are pulled back but the following palatal consonant is also pulled forward. I have several examples in my data
where the palatal /j/ in *year* is pulled forwards towards the alveo-
palatal region and becomes fricative, yielding the form [ˈðɪʃːɪə]. This
form only occurs where there is no stress on the word *year*—when *year*
has already been mentioned and can be readily understood in the
context in which it is spoken.* One must suppose that the reason
why initial consonants are so rarely obviously changed by assimilatory
processes is that syllable initial consonants play a much more important part in identifying a word than do syllable final consonants.
The last two examples both involve /m/ as the word final consonant.
In 15 /m/ is realized before /f/ as a labio-dental nasal [ɱ]—
pronounced with the upper teeth biting into the lower lip, just as
they do in pronouncing /f/. A similar realization of /m/ can often
be observed in words like *symphony* and *emphasis*. In 16 /m/ is realized as a velar nasal before the velar stop /g/. I have only observed
this particular phenomenon in connection with the form *I'm*—it also
occurs frequently in forms like *I'm coming, I'm conscious, I'm grateful.*

It is very important in trying to reproduce examples of assimilation
of the sort I have shown here that the total speech context in which
they are produced is borne in mind. In all cases they were produced
in a larger context than that shown here, by a speaker speaking
reasonably fluently. In this context, in a normal situation, they would
certainly not be remarked. They always occur in the least obvious
part of the syllable—the final position. They are quite obscure compared with the explicitly pronounced initial consonants and the
vowels of stressed syllables. I have already suggested that in listening
to spoken English the native speaker concentrates on the stressed
syllables. It is interesting to see that in general the *type* of articulation
of any syllable final consonant is preserved as is also the *voicing* value.
(The latter fact should be especially noted by speakers of languages
like German, Polish and Greek where the voicing value for word
final consonants is subject to assimilatory rules and will be governed
by the voicing value for the initial consonant of the following word.)
Within the set of stops and nasals the labial and velar value of the
final consonant is preserved. It is only the dental set /t, d, n/ which
is generally eligible for assimilation. We shall find these consonants
very widely involved in other simplifying processes.

*Gordon Walsh points out to me that for him *yearly* rhymes with *early* not *clearly.*
For such a speaker the phonemic form of *yearly* should be /ˈjɜlɪ/. See further
discussion on page 81.

4.2 Elision

Another very common process in informal speech is elision—the 'missing out' of a consonant or vowel, or both, that would be present in the slow colloquial pronunciation of a word in isolation. As with assimilation the most common place to find consonant elision is at the end of a syllable. The most common consonants to find involved in elision are /t/ and /d/. We shall begin by considering examples involving the elision of /t/:

1	/'fɜst'θri/	['fɜs'θri]	first three
2	/'lɑst'jɪə/	['lɑs'jɪə]	last year
3	/məʊst'risənt/	[məʊs'risənt]	most recent
4	/'ɪntərest'reɪts/	['ɪntres'reɪts]	interest rates
5	/'west'dʒɜmən/	['wes'dʒɜmən]	West German
6	/ðə'fæktðət/	[ðə'fækðət]	the fact that
7	/'æspekts/	['æspeks]	aspects
8	/'kɒnflɪktstɪl/	['kɒnflɪkstɪl]	conflict still
9	/'mʌstbɪ/	['mʌsbɪ]/['mʌspɪ]	must be
10	/'prəʊtest'mitɪŋ/	['prəʊtes'mitɪŋ]	protest meeting
11	/'ɪntərestəvðə/	['ɪntresəðə]	interest of the

Examples 1–10 all show the elision of /t/ when it occurs between two consonants. This process is so common that one is surprised to hear a /t/ in the stream of speech in this position. In scores of examples of *West German* and *West Germany* in my data I can find none where a medial /t/ is heard. This is a well established habit even in quite slow and deliberate speech. The last example, 11, shows the elision of /t/ following /s/ and before an unstressed vowel. This sort of elision is not as general as that exemplified in numbers 1–10 but it is certainly not rare.

/d/ elides even more readily than /t/ and in more environments. Here are examples involving the elision of /d/:

1	/'wɜld'waɪld'laɪf'fʌnd/	['wɜl'waɪ'laɪ'fʌnd]	World Wild Life Fund
2	/dɪs'tʃɑdʒd'prɪzənəz/	[dɪs'tʃɑdʒ'prɪzənəz]	discharged prisoners
3	/'aɪələnd'trʌbl̩'z/	[ɑːlən'trʌbl̩z]	(Northern) Ireland troubles
4	/'hɜld'twentɪ/	['hɜl'twentɪ]	hurled twenty (yards)
5	/'nʌθɪŋ'stændz'stɪl/	['nʌθɪŋ'stæn'stɪl]	nothing stands still

6 /ˈfɔˈθaʊzəndwə/   [ˈfɔˈθaʊzənwə]   four thousand
were

7 /ˈlændɪdˈnəʊzˈfɜst/   [ˈlændɪˈnəʊzˈfɜst]   landed nose
first

8 /hudˈbinɒnˈdjutɪ/   [huˈbinɒnˈdʒutɪ]   who'd been on
duty

9 /səˈspendɪdfrəm/   [səˈspendɪfrəm]   suspended
from

10 /ˈræpɪdlɪ/   [ˈræpɪlɪ]   rapidly

11 /ˈʃɪpsˈlaʊdˈspikə/   [ˈʃɪpsˈlaʊˈspikə]   ship's
loudspeaker

12 /ðətðeəkʊdbɪ/   [ðəʔðəkʊbɪ]   that there could
be

13 /əzkənˈfjʊzdəzˈevə/   [əzknˈfjuzəzˈevə]   as confused as
ever

14 /ˈgraʊndˈpreʃə/   [ˈgraʊmˈpreʃə]   ground
pressure

15 /ˈbændfəˈlaɪf/   [ˈbæmfəˈlaɪf]   banned for life

Examples 1–6 are just like the majority of the /t/ elision examples—they involve the loss of /d/ in a syllable final sequence, preceding another consonant. These represent a very common elision process. Notice that in examples 2 and 4 where the /d/ of the participle is elided in the informal form. This marker is very generally elided. In examples 3 and 4 where /d/ is elided before a /t/ it should not be supposed that the vowels in the preceding syllables shorten, in the way that they would be short and followed by a glottal stop before a final /t/. The vowel and /n/ in 3 and the /l/ in 4 retain the length that they would have had before /d/.

Examples 7–12 all involve the elision of /d/ before a consonant but immediately following a vowel. We have no examples of /t/ eliding in this context. These examples where /d/ is elided following a vowel need to be reproduced with a considerable difference between the prominent stressed syllables and the very obscure unstressed syllables in order to recapture the effect of the original (see p. 68) for example).

Example 13 shows /d/ elided following a consonant and preceding a vowel—very like example 11 of /t/ elision.

Examples 14 and 15 are just like examples 1–6; they involve elision of /d/ between two consonants but, in addition, the nasal preceding /d/ has undergone an assimilatory process of labialization, yielding [mp] and [ɱf].

The elision of /t/ and /d/ is by far the most common elision process. Indeed, as I have already suggested, it is more common for /t/ and /d/ to be elided between consonants than it is for them to be pronounced. There are other consonants which are much less regularly elided but whose elision is nonetheless by no means a rare event. It is clearly possible for any consonant to be elided in certain circumstances but I have only listed here forms which occurred quite frequently. These involve /v, ð, l, r, n/ and /k/.

Here are some examples of the elision of /v/:

1 /'faɪv'pi'em'njuz/	['faɪː'pi'em'njuz]	five p.m. news
2 /'ʃeəzhəvbin/	['ʃeːzəbɪn]*	shares have been
3 /wivbinkən'sɪdərɪŋ/	[wɪbɪŋkən'sɪdrɪŋ]	we've been considering
4 /əv'kɔs/	[ə'kɔs]	of course
5 /'nidzəvðə/	['nizəðə]	needs of the
6 /'tʃɪldrən'liv'skul/	['tʃɪldrən'liː'skul]	children leave school

Examples 2–5 here represent the most frequent types of /v/ elision. When /v/ is the final consonant in an unstressed grammatical form like *of* and *have* and immediately precedes another consonant, it is very often elided. Notice that in example 5 this elision† gives rise to a form that might out of context be interpreted as *knees of the (working people)*. In the context of the report of speech by a Trade Union leader attacking the government of the day, the only possible interpretation is *needs of the working people*. Examples 1 and 6, where a /v/ which is the final consonant in a stressed lexical item is elided, occur less frequently but are by no means rare. I have transcribed the vowel in the phonetic brackets in each of these examples followed by a length mark [ː]. This mark simply indicates that the vowel retains the length that it would have had before a voiced consonant even though the consonant itself is elided.

Examples of the elision of /ð/ are similarly restricted:

1 /aɪ'θɪŋkðətwəz/	[ʌ'θɪŋkətwəz]	I think that was
2 /'wentðə'weɪəvðə/	['wentə'weɪːðə]	went the way of the

* In order to avoid introducing another symbol, I have retained [e] in the phonetic transcription. Throughout the exemplification this should be taken as symbolizing a quality nearer to Cardinal Vowel 3 [ɛ] than to Cardinal Vowel 2 [e].

† See the section on the elision of /d/ on pages 66–7.

3 /əndðə'məʊməntwʌnz/	[n̩ð'məʊməntwʌnz]	and the moment one's (back is turned)
4 /təwɪð'drɔfrəmðə'hɒspɪtəl/	[twɪð'drɔfrəmə'hɒsp-ɪtl]	to withdraw from the hospital
5 /'nɔðən'aɪələnd/	['nɔːn'ɑːlənd]	Northern Ireland

2–4 all exemplify the same process, the form of the definite article being realized as [ə]. In all these cases the definiteness of the noun is clearly established and phonetic [ə] can only be interpreted as realizing the form /ðə/. Example 5 is a really quite rare *type* of simplification though this particular instance can be found in very many news broadcasts since Northern Ireland has been very frequently in the news.

Here are some examples of the elision of /l/:

1 /'ɔlsəʊ/	['ɔsəʊ]	also
2 /'ɔlredɪ/	['ɔredɪ]	already
3 /'rɔjəl'grin'dʒækɪts/	['rɔː'grin'dʒækɪts]	Royal Green Jackets
4 /'ɔlðə'sɪtɪzənz/	['ɔðə'sɪtɪzənz]	all the citizens
5 /'sɜtənlɪ/	['sɜtənɪ]	certainly
6 /ən'əʊld'mɪl/	[ən'əʊd'mɪl]	an old mill
7 /'kʌlmɪneɪtɪd/	['kʌmɪneɪtɪd]	culminated

Examples 1–4 represent a very general process in modern spoken English—the loss of /l/ following the vowel /ɔ/. This process is of course historically established in words like *talk* and *walk*. Even in slow colloquial English, words beginning with *all*—*altogether, all right, always*—are very frequently pronounced without an /l/ following the /ɔ/. Examples 3 and 4 show this process applied more generally. 5 is an example of the loss of /l/ in the suffix *-ly*. It occurs quite frequently in *certainly* and more rarely in forms like *mysteriously, charmingly*. It is possible that examples 6 and 7 should not be dealt with under the heading of 'elision'. Certainly no /l/ is heard in these examples. On the other hand the vowel preceding elided /l/ in each case has the sort of 'dark' resonance that one associates with vowels preceding syllable final /l/s. Both of these last examples occur in really quite rapid speech.

Examples of /r/ elision are less frequent than examples of /l/ elision.

1 /ə'jiərə'gəʊ/	[ə'jɜː'gəʊ]	a year ago
2 /ɪn'vaɪərənmənt/	[ɪn'vɑːmnt]	environment
3 /'jʊrə'pɪən/	['jɜː'pɪən]	European
4 /'terərɪst/	['teːrɪst]	terrorist
5 /'θæŋkverɪ'mʌtʃ/	['θæŋkveː'mʌtʃ]	(to) thank very much
6 /fər'ɪnstənts/	['fɪnstənts]	for instance
7 /'kʌmfrəm'sʌm/	['kʌmfəm'sʌm]	come from some (distance)
8 /kɑntrɪ'membə/	[kɑntɪ'membə]	can't remember

Examples 1–4 all show loss of /r/ immediately following a stressed syllable where /r/ is initial in an unstressed syllable /rə/. In each case not only does /r/ become elided but also the vowel /ə/. The preceding stressed vowel is lengthened in each case. One might suggest that the length of time taken to pronounce the stressed syllable + lengthened vowel is about equivalent to that taken for the pronunciation of the stressed syllable + unstressed syllable /rə/. 5 is very similar except that the syllable preceding /r/ is unstressed and the following unstressed vowel is /ɪ/ not /ə/. Examples 6 and 7 both show loss of /r/ in a grammatical word in an unstressed syllable. In the case of 6 the loss of /ər/ seems to result in the /f/ being brought forward as initial consonant in the following stressed syllable. This is not quite accurate however because the /f/ in this position is not as strongly fricative or as long as an /f/ initial in a stressed syllable like *fin* would be. I did consider transcribing the reduced form like this: [f'ɪnstənts]. This has the disadvantage of suggesting that the /f/ is disassociated from the first syllable which ought to imply that the /f/ itself is syllabic. In the example I am dealing with here the /f/ does not have syllabic value. It is a weak onset to the syllable in which it appears. So I leave the rather misleading transcription and add this explanatory note. The final example, number 8, shows the loss of /r/ in unstressed initial position in a lexical word. This is not uncommon in words like *remove, resolve, require* when they occur in the middle of a quite long utterance.

Just as we found in discussing the elision of /l/, that even though no /l/ was pronounced, the preceding vowel still had the 'dark' resonance associated with syllable final /l/, so we find the same sort of thing with the elision of /n/. When /n/ is elided an adjacent vowel is likely to be nasalized. Even though the consonant /n/ is not realized as an individual segment it nonetheless leaves its traces in the word. Let us consider some examples of /n/ elision:

1 /ɪnðə'faɪnələ'nælɪsɪs/	[ĩðəfaɪnlə'nælɪsɪs]	in the final analysis
2 /bɪ'twɪnðətu/	[bɪ'twĩðətu]	between two (ministers)
3 /'mitɪŋɪn'rəʊm/	['mitɪŋĩ'rəʊm]	meeting in Rome
4 /wʌn'wɒntstə'meɪk/	[wʌ̃'wɒ̃stə'meɪk]	one wants to make
5 /'kɒnstəntlɪ/	[kɒ̃stəntlɪ]	constantly
6 /ɪtsɪnðə'fɔm/	[tsĩðə'fɔm]	it's in the form
7 'nəʊntəðə'pʌblɪk/	[nə̃ʊtθ'pʌblɪk]	known to the public

Here we see that /n/ can be elided, but leave a nasalized vowel, in final position both in stressed syllables (examples 2, 4, 5, 7), and in unstressed syllables (examples 1, 3, 4, 6). The only requirement seems to be that /n/ should be followed by another consonant either in the same syllable or in the next syllable. In each case it is the vowel preceding the elided /n/ which is nasalized.

Whereas all speakers exhibit regular elision of /t/ and /d/, and most speakers exhibit occasional elision of /ð, v/ and /l/, the elision of /n/ varies very much more between speakers. Some speakers exhibit very frequent examples of /n/ elision with vowel nasalization. Such speakers often have a nasal resonance in all the vowels which occur near nasal consonants and elide other nasal consonants besides /n/—for example, *there seems to be* may be realized as [ðe'sĩztəbɪ]. Such speakers may be said to have a predominantly *nasal setting*. Other speakers do not have this setting, and elision of /n/ is rare in their speech.

Elision of /k/ seems to occur regularly only in a very few forms:

1 /'ɑsktɪm/	['ɑstɪm]	asked him
2 /ɪk'spektɪd/	[ɪ'spektɪd]	expected
3 /ɪk'skɜʃən/	[ɪ'skɜʃn̩]	excursion
4 /ɪk'strɔdɪnərɪ/	[ɪ'strɔdn̩rɪ]	extraordinary

The past form of *ask* frequently turns up with elided /k/. Forms beginning with unstressed *ex-* sometimes have an elided /k/, especially when the word has already been mentioned or is highly predictable in the context it occurs in. For example in one news broadcast, the commencement of a new series of day excursions organized by British Rail is announced. The first sentence of this news item contains the full form of *excursion*—/ɪkˈskɜʃən/ but in subsequent sentences the reduced form appears.

In some of the examples we have looked at so far there are instances of vowel elision which I have passed silently by. For example under the elision of /n/ we find example 7:

/ˈnəʊntəðəˈpʌblɪk/ [ˈnə̃ʊtθˈpʌblɪk] known to the public

The consonant sequence [tθp] is created by the elision of the vowel /ə/ in /ðə/ and the subsequent syllabification and devoicing of /ð/ to [θ]. Vowel elision is a very frequent process and very often occurs together with other processes involving assimilation, syllabification and the elision of consonants. We shall begin by looking at examples of single words which simply involve elision of a vowel:

1 /ˈɪntərəst/	[ˈɪntrəst]	interest
2 /ˈdɪfərənt/	[ˈdɪfrənt]	different
3 /kəˈlektɪv/	[ˈklektɪv]	collective
4 /pəˈlɪtɪkəl/	[ˈplɪtɪkl]	political
5 /fəˈnætɪks/	[ˈfnætɪks]	fanatics
6 /ˈtɔkətɪv/	[ˈtɔktɪv]	talkative
7 /ˈkæbɪnət/	[ˈkæbnət]	cabinet
8 /ˈmɪnɪstə/	[ˈmɪnstə]	minister
9 /ˈtʃansɪlə/	[ˈtʃanslə]	chancellor
10 /ˈsɪmɪlə/	[ˈsɪmlə]	similar

The first two examples are typical of a large class of English words which are well known to allow the loss of an unstressed /ə/ vowel. The second, informal, pronunciation is often allowed as an alternative pronunciation in pronouncing dictionaries. In this class what is usually involved is an initial stressed syllable whose shape is unaffected by the elision and two or more unstressed syllables containing /ə/ or /ɪ/ vowels. Other well known words in this class are *secretary*, *library*, *governor*, *prisoner* which are often pronounced [ˈsekrətrɪ], [ˈlaɪbrɪ], [ˈgʌvnə], [ˈprɪznə] when they occur in longer utterances. The next three examples, 3–5, are not normally allowed as alternative pronunciations by pronouncing dictionaries but occur frequently even in quite slow formal speech and very frequently in informal speech. These examples involve the loss of an unstressed /ə/ in the initial syllable of a word and the consequent moving up of the initial consonant in the unstressed syllable to form part of a cluster with the initial consonant of the stressed syllable. In example 5 this provides the first 'impossible' consonant cluster that we have met in the data so far. By the rules for syllable initial clusters that we observed in 2.4, the initial cluster /fn/ was excluded. We merely note the occurrence of this 'impossible' cluster at this point and return to discuss the problems raised by this and similar sequences later. Example 6, involving the loss of /ə/, and 7–10, involving the loss of unstressed /ɪ/, all lose an unstressed medial vowel in a word of the structure stress-unstress-unstress.

We will now turn to look at the same sort of process, simple vowel elision unaccompanied by assimilation or syllabification, occurring in sequences of words:

1	/ˈtutəˈθri/	[ˈtutˈθri]	two to three
2	/ˈbæktəˈlʌndən/	[ˈbæktˈlʌndn̩]	back to London
3	/təˈmit/	[ˈtmit]	to meet
4	/ˈaftərˈɔl/	[ˈaftˈrɔl]	after all
5	/ðɪsaftəˈnun/	[ðɪsaftˈnun]	this afternoon
6	/ɪnəˈfæʃənwɪtʃ/	[ɪnˈfæʃn̩wɪtʃ]	in a fashion which
7	/ˈkʌmtəðɪˈendəv/	[ˈkʌmtðɪjˈendəv]	come to the end of
8	/ˈfjʊtjəkəˈrɪə/	[ˈfjʊtʃkəˈrɪə]	future career
9	/ɪtsðəˈweɪ/	[tsðəˈweɪ]	it's the way
10	/ˈəʊvəðəˈjɪəz/	[ˈəʊvðəˈjɜz]	over the years
11	/ˈgəʊɪŋtbɪˈkʌm/	[ˈgɜŋtbɪˈkʌm]	going to become
12	/əˈwikɔˈtuəˈgəʊ/	[əˈwikˈtuˈgəʊ]	a week or two ago

May I remind the reader that in order to recreate these examples as plausible pieces of spoken English, which would not even be observed as 'oddly' pronounced, the examples must be placed in an extended context. So number 12, which seems very unlikely taken, as it were, in cold blood, must be inserted into a sentence like *He was last seen a week or two ago and then appeared to be in the best of health*, spoken reasonably fluently.

Many of these examples, 1–5, 7 and 11, involve loss of /ə/ in the unstressed syllable /tə/ when the following syllable begins with a consonant. This is a very common pattern. Note that the loss of shwa /ə/ in 3 produces an 'impossible' initial sequence, /tm/. Another 'impossible' sequence is produced by the loss of initial /ɪ/ in example 9. Very many sentences beginning with *it's* occur in my data and in the majority of these the initial /ɪ/ is elided when the sentence runs on without a marked pause after the previous sentence—when the sentence is internal in a 'spoken paragraph'. Often the syllabicity of the

/ɪ/ is, as it were, transferred to the /s/ yielding forms like the following:

1 /ɪtskən'sɪdəd/   [tṣkṇ'sɪdəd]   it's considered
2 /ɪts'nɒt/   [tṣ'nɒt]   it's not
3 /ɪts'prɒbəblɪ/   [tṣ'prɒbəblɪ]   it's probably

Sometimes the 'syllabicity' of the initial syllable is lost altogether as in example 9. Sometimes the /t/ of the first syllable is elided as well, yielding forms like: [ṣkṇ'sɪdəd], [ṣ'nɒt], [ṣ'prɒbəblɪ] where the [s] may either keep the syllabicity, or, in a more reduced form, lose it and simply become part of the initial cluster of the first syllable: [skṇ'sɪdəd], ['snɒt], ['sprɒbəblɪ].

In the teaching of pronunciation we tend to stress that in spoken English, unlike Slavic and Germanic languages, there is no assimilation of voicing or voicelessness across word boundaries. So in English, given a sequence like /'bɪgpə'reɪd/ there is no possibility of the /g/ being realized as [k] before the voiceless /p/. This is in general true, and it is certainly important to insist on it in teaching pronunciation. If we are simply observing how native English speakers speak, we will find that we need to modify this sweeping statement a little. Consider the following examples:

1 /'səʊldtəðə'pʌblɪk/   ['səʊltθ'pʌblɪk]   sold to the public
2 /bɪ'kɒz/   ['pkɒz]   because
3 /'bæŋkəv'ɪŋglənd/   ['bæŋkf'ɪŋglənd]   Bank of England
4 /ðə'fɜst'raʊnd/   ['θfɜs'raʊnd]   the first round
5 /dɪk'teɪtɪŋ/   [tḳ'teɪtɪŋ]   dictating
6 /'ðætsðə'njuz/   ['ðætsθ'njuz]   that's the news

Here we find 'voiced' consonants which occur in unstressed syllables in grammatical words becoming 'voiceless' when, as a result of the elision of /ə/ they occur next to a 'voiceless' consonant. This process is particularly common where the words *the* and *of* are involved—see the examples, 1, 3, 4 and 6. A similar process occurs, but much more rarely, within words when a /ə/ is lost and the 'voiced' initial consonant of an unstressed syllable occurs next to a 'voiceless' consonant—see examples 2 and 5. (It may not be clear how to interpret the phonetic transcription in square brackets of example 5. The syllabic diacritic beneath [k] indicates a comparatively long period of closure here. A small burst of aspiration follows the release of the initial [t]—not, I think, sufficient to justify transcribing it as a voiceless vowel.)

There are very few examples in my data of an assimilation of *manner* of articulation of consonants—not enough to state any sort of general conclusion. One form however occurs frequently—and this is hardly surprising in view of the fact that my data includes news broadcasts and discussions—and that is the form ['gʌbmn̩t] for *government*. It's perfectly possible to find 'intermediate' forms between this and /gʌvənmənt/— ['gʌvəmənt] and ['gʌvm̩n̩t] but the form which occurs most frequently is ['gʌbmn̩t].

The next set of examples is an assortment consisting of elisions involving more than just a vowel or just a consonant in each case. Elisions of this sort are very common and I can do no more than exemplify some common types here:

1 /'praɪsɪzənd'ɪŋkʌmz/	['praɪsn̩'ɪŋkʌmz]	prices and incomes
2 /sək'sidɪnɪm'pəʊzɪŋ/	[s̩k'sidm̩'pəʊzɪŋ]	succeed in imposing
3 /pə'hæps/	['pæps]	perhaps
4 /ɪn'ðɪs'kaɪndəv-'prezən'teɪʃən/	[n̩'ðɪs'kaɪn-'prezn̩'teɪʃn̩]	in this kind of presentation
5 /pə'tɪkjuləlɪ/	[pə'tɪklɪ]	particularly
6 /'æktjuəlɪ/	['ækʃlɪ]	actually
7 /'əʊɪŋtʊ/	['əʊnə]	owing to
8 /'gəʊɪŋtəbɪ/	['gənəbɪ]	going to be
9 /wɪlhəvbɪn/	[wɪləbɪn]	will have been
10 /ɪk'strɔdɪnərɪ/	['strɔnrɪ]	extraordinary

Many of these examples will appear to be very undesirable types of pronunciation if they are allowed to be at all prominent in the stream of speech! Students should certainly not be encouraged to mimic them. What they should be encouraged to do is to study a taped news broadcast and see if they can find similar features.

There are a few generalizations that can be made about these assorted examples. With the single exception of ['pæps] no stressed syllable is affected by elision—what tends to happen is that a series of unstressed syllables is run together. 7, 8 and 9 each illustrate a very common phrase consisting of grammatical words. The form represented by the transcription in square brackets is very frequently found in informal speech—again in obscure places, never in prominent places in the utterance. The last example, number 10, illustrates the sort of thing that often happens to polysyllabic words beginning with *ex-*. Just as the form *it's* is often simplified to [ts] or [ts̩] and, further, to [s̩] or [s], so /ɪks/ is often simplified to [ks̩] or [ks], [s̩] or [s] as in:

1 /ɪk'strimlɪ/	[kṣ'trimlɪ]	extremely
2 /ɪk'spleɪnd/	[ṣ'pleɪnd]	explained
3 /ɪk'saɪtɪd/	['ksaɪtɪd]	excited
4 /ɪk'spləʊʒən/	['spləʊʒn̩]	explosion

These last examples, as with other examples that we have noted but not stopped to consider, may present us with 'impossible' initial consonant sequences. In the constraints on initial sequences of consonants in English words that we examined in 2.4 the only initial clusters involving voiceless stops (other than those with /w, l, r/), were where /s/ was the first element of the cluster—as in *stream, scout* and *sprawl*. Yet, as we have seen, we can find utterances beginning with [tm] as in ['tmit] *to meet*, with [tsn] as in ['tsnɒt] *it's not* and with [ks] as in ['ksaɪtɪd] *excited*. The foreign learner may well be bewildered by the apparent conflict between the statement of the regularities on the one hand and the phonetic facts that are described here on the other. Is he to suppose that the structural constraints are wrong and that any random sequence of consonants can occur initially in English as these observations tend to suggest? Clearly not, because a careful search through the initial consonant sequences of words listed in a pronouncing dictionary in their slow colloquial form will not reveal any sequences that contravene the regularities stated in Chapter 2. We must be careful to draw a distinction between the 'idealized', slow colloquial form and the phonetic facts of normal informal speech. The status of the statements of constraints on sequences of consonants is exactly like the description of the 'ideal' phoneme described as it might occur in isolation. These statements represent the sort of knowledge which a native speaker brings to bear in selecting the odd-numbered words in the following list as being acceptable English words but not the even-numbered words:

1 /spred/	(spread)
2 /tlingit/	
3 /bləʊ/	(blow)
4 /mbwa/	
5 /smɪə/	(smear)
6 /pkambg/	

Many of the phonetic forms that an English speaker actually produces in informal speech might appear to him as 'exotic', un-English forms if they were pronounced like slow colloquial forms. The whole point is that they are *not* 'ideal' citation forms of each word uttered maximally clearly and explicitly but they are sequences occurring in the stream of normal informal speech in non-prominent parts of the utterance. They represent the natural simplifying processes which occur in all languages.

We may note in passing here that not all accents of English simplify in the same way. Consider a form like *mister*. Some accents of English will tend to simplify the consonant cluster here and produce a form ['mɪsə]—many Irish speakers, for instance, produce a form like this. RP on the whole tends to elide the vowel of the initial syllable yielding ['mstə], ['pstə] or even ['stə].

4.3 Word boundary markers

When words are pronounced in isolation, or even in short groups in slow colloquial style, there are several phonetic cues which signal the beginnings and ends of words. When they occur in stressed syllables, initial 'voiceless' stops are marked by aspiration, initial fricatives are marked by greater relative friction than occurs in other environments, initial /l/ is marked by being 'clearer' than it is word finally. In final position the presence of a 'voiceless' stop either by itself or in a cluster is marked by a glottal stop. There are many discussions in the literature about how clues like these may be used to distinguish sequences of words which consist of a sequence of identical segments. Thus the sequence of phonemes in /waɪtʃuz/ may represent both *why choose* and *white shoes*. The difference between them may be represented by the insertion of a stress marker yielding /waɪ'tʃuz/ as against /'waɪt'ʃuz/. The phonetic clues which enable us to distinguish between them include greater length in the vowel of *why* as against less length and the vowel cut off by a glottal stop in *white*. In informal speech these markers are very frequently obscured to some extent.

Similarly if two words occur in the stream of speech, the first one ending with the same consonant that the second one begins with, the word boundary between the two will be marked in slow colloquial speech by a 'geminated' or double consonant. The juncture between *polite* and *terms* in /pəlaɪttɜmz/ will be phonetically marked by a 'geminated' or double consonant: [pə'laɪtːʰɜmz]. Since such consonants never occur internally to a word in English except in the case of a compound word formed by the junction of two lexical items as in *bus-stop*, *rock cake*, *penknife* they only and always serve to mark word boundaries. In informal speech the compound words, *bus-stop* etc. quickly lose the geminated consonant and very often other word final word initial sequences of identical consonants lose their geminated

consonants too. The following typical examples of this lack of
gemination occur in my data—notice that they often involve loss of /t/
or /d/:

1 /'tɔkttu/	['tɔktə]	talked to
2 /ɒnmæn'hætən/	[ɒmæn'hætn̩]	on Manhattan
3 /ət'tʃekəz/	[ə'tʃekəz]	at Chequers
4 /ɪtkən/	[ɪkən]	it can

This sort of loss will hardly cause any surprise since it is in many
cases exactly the sort of loss we have already considered under the
heading of 'elision' of /t/ or /d/. It is mentioned again here in order
to stress the fact that gemination is a word boundary marker and the
loss of this constitutes a loss of information about where the word
boundaries are.

4.4 Consonants and vowels in the stream of speech

In Chapter 3, in discussing some of the ways in which unstressed
syllables typically differ from stressed syllables, I mentioned that one
common variable is the difference in explicit pronunciation of consonants in initial position in stressed and unstressed syllables. I said
there that this difference in explicitness is present in slow colloquial
pronunciation as well as in informal speech. In informal speech the
difference between the explicitly pronounced consonants and other
consonants is particularly marked. I have already mentioned the difficulties we meet as soon as we try to transcribe 'weakened'
consonants. If, for example, I transcribe the medial consonant in
worker with an [x] where [x] has the IPA* value for a voiceless, fricative, velar consonant this symbol implies a 'proper', audible, velar
fricative. What I want to suggest is a weakened [k] where the back
of the tongue just fails to make contact with the velum, thus allowing
a little air to pass through the remaining gap. It has none of the
length and robust friction that one associates with the 'cardinal' symbol [x]. Nonetheless I am going to give some examples of 'weakened'
consonants, and in order to make it quite clear where the weakening
lies I am going to transcribe these 'weakened' consonants with symbols adapted from the IPA alphabet. In the examples the 'weakened'
consonants are all stops. As we have seen, some obscure fricatives,
/v/ and /ð/ especially, become elided and /l, r/ and /n/ can also
be elided. Those examples of these consonants which are not elided,
like the remaining fricatives and /m/, are simply pronounced in a

* Alphabet of the International Phonetic Association.

shorter, weaker manner. I have no way of showing this in transcription without introducing a large number of symbols and diacritics. We shall have to take the set of stops as representative of this weakening process. In the transcription the unfamiliar symbols have the following values:

[ɸ] weakened /p/
[s̞] weakened /t/—much less fricative and high pitched than [s]
[x] weakened [k]
[β] weakened /b/
[z̞] weakened /d/—much less fricative than [z]
[ɣ] weakened /g/

1 /bɪkəz/	[pxəz]	because
2 /'lʊkðeə/	['lʊxðeː]	look there
3 /sʌm'taɪməgəʊ/	[sʌm'taɪməɣəʊ]	some time ago
4 /'trækɪŋ'deɪtə/	['træxɪŋ'deɪs̞ə]	tracking data
5 /kəm'plɪtɪd/	[km'plɪs̞ɪd]	completed
6 /'gəʊŋ'bæktuaʊə'mæp]	['gɔŋ'bæxtwɑ'mæp]	going back to our map
7 /'sætɪsfaɪd/	['sæs̞sfaɪd]	satisfied
8 /wɪvbin/	[wɪvβɪn]	we've been
9 /mʌstbi/	[mʌsβɪ]	must be
10 /pə'lɪtɪkəl/	[ɸə'lɪtɪk̩]	political
11 /'lʊkɪŋtə'faɪnd/	['lʊxɪŋtə'faɪnd]	looking to find
12 /'spəʊksmən/	['spəʊxsmən]	spokesman
13 /'nɒtgəʊɪŋtəbɪ/	['nɒtɣɔŋs̞əbɪ]	*not* going to be
14 /hɪzbin'traɪɪŋ/	[hɪzβɪn'trɑːŋ]	he's been trying
15 /ɔl'redɪ/	[ɔ'rez̞ɪ]	already

This sort of 'weakening' is very common. The most frequent examples are of 'weakening' of /k/ and /t/. The general requirement seems to be simply that the consonant should not be initial in a stressed syllable. Weak consonants can occur either in the environment of other consonants—as in 1, 2 and 6 for example—or between vowels as in 3, 5 and 15. I have made no attempt to distinguish between consonants that are final in a stressed syllable and consonants that are initial in an unstressed syllable—I have classed them together as 'weak'. In example number 5, *completed*, there seems to me little point in discussing whether /t/ is final in /plit/ as the morphology would suggest or initial in /tɪd/. My general impression is that if native English speakers are asked to pronounce a word syllable by syllable they will tend to produce syllables of the structure consonant-vowel wherever possible. This would lead us to expect [kəm-'pli-tɪd]. However people have very personal ideas about how they syllabify words and it is by no means always clear what these ideas are based on. For practical teaching purposes, at least, I think it is more useful to distinguish between 'strong' stressed syllable in-itial consonants and 'weak' consonants which occur elsewhere than to worry about syllable division.

The vowels of English are usually characterized in terms of four basic variables—tongue height in mouth on a scale close-open, area of greatest stricture between the hump of the tongue and the roof of the mouth on a scale front-back, the posture of the lips in terms of rounded-unrounded and finally whether the vowel retains a stable quality throughout its articulation. These vowels represent the 'ideal' set of vowels which an RP speaker can produce in slow colloquial, maximally explicit speech. There are two reasons why the form of the vowels described in Chapter 2 may be modified in the stream of speech. One is that vowels in unstressed syllables will tend to simplify and the other is that some vowels seem to be particularly vulnerable to a change in quality even in stressed syllables. It may well be that this vulnerability occurs because of the constant pressure of sound change in the language. Historically the vowels of English have un-dergone many changes and there is every reason to suppose that the process is going on now as it were 'under our noses'. Some of the tendencies I mention here may become established in the course of time. Then the description of the vowels in isolation will have to be modified. Other tendencies may be merely temporary fashions which will disappear again. We have no way of knowing which tendencies will be established and which will disappear. It does however seem reasonable to guess, where a vowel belongs to a set of vowels whose other members have undergone a given process that has now become established, and we see tendencies for the same process to apply to the vowel we are interested in, that this tendency is very likely to become established. Consider for example the /r/ set of vowels. His-torically RP lost /r/ in final position and before a consonant and 'replaced' it with /ə/. Then a further process of simplification oc-curred and some of the vowels in the set lost the final /ə/ and 'replaced' it with vowel length. We can represent this process, with considerable simplification, like this:

-ir	ɪə	ɪə
-er	eə	eə
-ar	aə	[ɑː]—/ɑ/
-or	ɔə	[ɔː]—/ɔ/
-ur	ʊə	ʊə

Today we observe that many people have lost the distinction /ʊə/—/ɔ/ in words like *poor* and *paw*—the words are now homophones, pronounced identically, and the distinction is lost between /ʊə/ and /ɔ/. For many speakers phonetic [ʊə] is only preserved in triphthongs as in *curate, pure*—/'kjʊərət/, /'pjʊə/. Even this remnant has now disappeared in the speech of many speakers who pronounce these words /'kjɔrət/ and /'pjɔ/—again /ʊə/ falls together with /ɔ/.

This process has been observed to be encroaching now for some years (see for instance the discussion in Gimson, 1962: 139). A somewhat similar process is also very common and that is the simplification of /eə/ to [eː]. This is mentioned by Gimson (1962) as a feature of 'advanced RP' but it is very common now and occurs frequently in my data spoken by people whose brand of RP would not be held to be 'advanced'. Examples of this are:

1 /'weə/	['weː]	where
2 /əʊvə'ðeə/	[əʊvə'ðeː]	over there
3 /'ʃeəzhəvbin/	['ʃeːzəbɪn]	shares have been (falling)
4 /'keədfə/	['keːdfə]	cared for

The final member of this set, /ɪə/, seems to be maintaining its diphthongal realization more firmly than /eə/. There are however many examples in my data of the realization of /ɪə/ as a central vowel rather more front than that in *bird, fur* etc. I shall transcribe this with the symbol [ɜ̟].

1 /'rɪəlɪ/	['rɜ̟lɪ]	really
2 /'nɪərɪst/	['nɜ̟rəst]	nearest
3 /ðə'jɪəbɪ'fɔ/*	[ðə'jɜ̟bɪ'fɔ]	the year before
4 /ə'sɪərɪəs'æksɪdənt/	[ə'sɜ̟rjəs'æksɪdənt]	a serious accident

The quality of this vowel is sometimes indistinguishable from the realization of /ɜ/ as in *curl, bird, purr*.

The set of /r/ vowels illustrates the difficulty of confident prediction about the direction of sound change. We may expect to see the emergence of a series, all the members of which have lost the final 'shwa'—but we may be disappointed in the expectation! For the moment, the foreign student should at least be aware of these alternative possibilities of realization of this set of vowels.

The /ɜ/ vowel which occurs in *cur, sir* etc. results from the historical falling together of vowels before /r/, as is suggested by the spelling of the vowel in the words *bird, word, herd*. This vowel, like the other members of the /r/ set, can be realized as [ə] in unstressed syllables:

*See note on page 65.

1 /ɪtsrɪəlɪ'kwaɪt'dɪfɪkəlt/	[tsrəlɪ'kwaɪʔ'dɪfɪk-l̩t]	it's really quite difficult
2 /ðə'pleɪsweəhiwəz-'faʊnd/	[ðə'pleɪswəhiz'faʊnd]	the place where he was found
3 /'piplɑ/	['pipl̩ə]	people are
4 /wʌnɔ'tu/	[wʌnə'tu]	one or two
5 /ðeɪwɜtəbɪ/	[ðeɪwətəbɪ]	they were to be

As the discussion in Chapter 3 would lead us to expect, most of the examples of vowel reduction that we find are in the unstressed syllables of grammatical words.

Two of the /ʊ/-ending vowels are subject to quite wide variation in realization in stressed as well as in unstressed syllables. It is not easy to perceive an overall pattern in the variation in this set. Here are some typical examples of realizations of /aʊ/ and /əʊ/:

1 /naʊðət/	[nɑðət]	now that
2 /saʊθəv'ɪŋglənd/	[sɑθf'ɪŋglənd]	south of England
3 /gəʊld/	['gɜld]	gold
4 /'jesɔ'nəʊ/	['jesə'nɜ]	yes or no

Here are examples of the same vowels as initial elements followed by another vowel either in the same or a second syllable:

1 /'fɔ'paʊə'tɔks/	['fɔ'pɑ'tɔks]	Four Power talks
2 /'aʊə'streŋkθ/	[ɑ'streŋkθ]	our strength
3 /kəʊə'lɪʃən/	[kɜ'lɪʃn̩]	coalition
4 /'gəʊɪŋ'bæk/	['gɜŋ'bæk]	going back

/aʊ/ and /aʊə/ are frequently realized as [ɑ], and /əʊ/, /əʊə/ as [ɜ]. It is clear that in the examples here the quality of the initial element of the diphthong is retained and the second element obscured or lost.

/ju/ and /u/ remain fairly stable in stressed syllables. In unstressed syllables the following pattern of reduction appears in the vowels of this set:/ju/—[jʊ],/aʊ/—[ʌ],/əʊ/—[ə] and/u/—[ə] or [ʊ].

1 /ðə'fjurɪ'meɪnɪŋ/	[ðə'fjʊrɪ'meɪnɪŋ]	the few remaining
2 /'sihaʊðeɪl'bi/	['sihʌðel'bi]	see how they'll be
3 /səʊwiʃæl'si/	[səwɪʃl̩'si]	so we shall see
4 /'kʌmɪŋtuðɪ'end/	['kʌmɪŋtəðɪ'end]	coming to the end

The /ɪ/-ending set of vowels is relatively stable in stressed syllables. In unstressed syllables the pattern is /i/—[ɪ], /eɪ/—[e] and /aɪ/ to [ʌ]. /ɔɪ/ occurs in few words and I found no examples of the reduction of this vowel in my data. Here are examples of the reduction of the other members of the set:

1 /ðeə'sɪmztəbi/	[ðe'sĩztəbɪ]	there seems to be
2 /nɒtmeɪdenɪ'izɪə/	[nɒtmedenɪ'izjə]	not made any easier
3 /aɪ'kɑntbɪ'liv/	[ʌ'kɑnʔbɪ'liv]	I can't believe

When any member of the basic vowel series reduces, it reduces to [ə]. Examples:

1 /ɪts'nɒt/	[əts'nɒt]	it's not
2 /'gɪvəntuðem/	['gɪvn̩tðəm]	given to them (already)
3 /ðə'mɪnɪstəkæn-'tʃeɪndʒɪt/	[ðə'mɪn̩stəkən-'tʃeɪndʒɪt]	the minister can change it
4 /'pleɪsɒvdɪs'kʌʃən/	['pleɪsəvdɪs'kʌʃn̩]	place of discussion (in public life)
5 /ɪfðeəkʊdbi/	[fθekəbɪ]	if there could be
6 /dʌzðəkə'mjunɪtɪ/	[dəzðək'mjun̩tɪ]	does the community

It is quite normal for foreign students of English to be taught a set of 'weak forms'—grammatical words which may have a different quality of vowel in a stressed syllable from the one which occurs in an unstressed syllable. The examples we have just been examining, like /aɪ/—[ʌ], and /ðem/—[ðəm] as pronunciations of *I* and *them* respectively, are instances of such 'weak forms'. It is important however to be clear that every instance of a grammatical word in an unstressed syllable need not be accompanied by vowel reduction. In general, vowel reduction may be expected but there are many cases in the data transcribed in this chapter where not all potentially reducible vowels are in fact reduced.

4.5 Reduction in visual clues

We have looked at the variation in the phonetic realizations of consonants and vowels in different segmental and stress contexts in informal speech. We have considered this exclusively from the point of view of the variation in *sound* of vowels and consonants. I want now to consider the variation in the visual clues that a listener may expect if he is considering on the one hand slow colloquial pronunciation and on the other informal speech. One advantage that a student in Britain who is actually face to face with his lecturer has over a student who is listening to tapes is that he can see the face of the speaker. It seems likely that different people make different use of visual clues. Some people rely on them heavily and find it difficult to hold a conversation with someone they cannot see—others rely very much less heavily on such clues. Since foreign learners need all the help they can get in the form of aids to interpreting the spoken message it seems worthwhile drawing to their attention what visual clues to segmental quality they may expect to find in informal speech and what they may not expect to find. I have already suggested the importance of visual clues in indicating the occurrence of stressed syllables in speech.

Whereas in slow colloquial pronunciation there may be a considerable amount of vertical movement of the lower jaw—so that, for instance, the jaw moves up before the /b/ in *rubber,* stays closed, and then opens again—there is much less movement in informal speech. The jaw drops less for the vowels, and the /b/ itself may be realized by a very quick twitch of the lower lip which moves up to make a very rapid closure (it does not as we have already noted always get to a complete closure) and then moves slightly away for the following vowel. There may be no obvious movement of the jaw itself at all. The same remarks hold for the realization of /p/ and /m/ when they are not initial in a stressed syllable. There is very much less jaw and lip movement than in slow colloquial pronunciation—in all cases there may not be a complete closure of the two lips. There is usually complete closure of the lips before stressed vowels—but, again, the period of closure is very brief.

In slow colloquial speech there is no difficulty in identifying /p/s, /b/s and /m/s by simply looking at the speaker's face—every time his lips close and part again even though nothing can be heard, you know that the only possible sound he can be making is one of those three. In informal speech the same generalization can still be made—if the lips are approached to each other the sound must be one of those three—but there is a much less obvious signal to watch for.

Now consider the labio-dental fricatives /f, v/. In slow colloquial speech it is usually possible to see a definite jaw movement upwards for the stricture of the consonant and then down again. It is often possible, too, to see a slight pouting out of the lower lip and the middle part of the two front upper teeth as they bite inside the soft part of the lip. And the stricture may be maintained for a considerable period. In conversational speech, all that may be visible is a small gesture of the lower lip backwards to bring it closer to the front teeth—and it is not a maintained gesture—simply a pulling back of the bottom lip against the upper teeth and then an immediate move back again. There is no visible jaw movement at all.

We have discussed the vertical movements of the lips and jaw which may be very obvious in the slow colloquial pronunciation of labial and labio-dental consonants but are very much reduced in informal pronunciation. In general in slow colloquial pronunciation there is usually a perceptible vertical movement of the jaw when any consonant or consonant sequence is articulated. If you say *utter, udder, acting, Anna, easy,* for example, it is possible to see a distinct movement upwards of the jaw for the formation of the stricture and then a movement downwards again as it is released. In informal pronunciation there is usually very little, if any, perceptible jaw movement except for labial consonants. The jaw remains slightly open, and the tongue articulates in this fairly fixed area, and the only noticeable movement of the jaw is when it moves up slightly for the labial consonants /p/, /b/ and /m/. So it is worth while spending time learning to observe jaw and lip movements as they are a valuable clue to the set of consonants being articulated.

Now that we have five of the consonants characterized (/p, b, m, f, v/) in terms of lip and jaw movements, let us see what further help, in identifying consonants, lip movements can give. There are some speakers of English to whom the following remarks do not apply— these are people who, even in very slow and careful speech, do not protrude or round their lips. For most speakers, however, some or all of the following remarks apply.

/w/ as initial in words like *window* and *wool* has close lip rounding in slow colloquial pronunciation. The lips are drawn forward and pursed round a small central opening—just about big enough to insert a pencil into. The corners of the mouth are drawn forward and the surface of both lips is wrinkled. In informal speech this very obvious rounding does not occur. The corners of the mouth and the lips are pushed very slightly forwards and the lips make a slight gesture towards each other in the vertical plane—the lips do not come as close together as they do for /p, b, m/ and the lower lip does not make the slight backward gesture as for /v/. For many speakers there is no external sign of /w/ except when it is initial in stressed words. If you pretend for a moment that you are a ventriloquist, and utter the sentence *We'll watch the window* without moving your lips, you will find that your /w/s can sound perfectly normal—it is a very different matter with /p/s and /b/s!

Similarly in slow colloquial pronunciation there is often a labial accompaniment to /s, z/ and to /ʃ, ʒ, tʃ, dʒ, r/. In the pronunciation of /s/ and /z/ this consists of a slight drawing forward of the corners of the mouth and a slight protrusion of the lower lip. In the pronunciation of /ʃ, ʒ, tʃ, dʒ/, it consists of a pushing forward of the corners of the mouth and considerable pouting of both upper and lower lips. By 'pouting' as opposed to 'rounding', I mean that the lips are pushed forward and out, so that some of the soft inside is exposed, not that they are drawn in round a central opening. In the slow colloquial pronunciation of /r/ as in *rum* there is often a pushing forward of the corners of the mouth together with slight pouting of the lower lip, and a very slight pouting of the upper lip. All these labial signs may be absent in informal speech. In the speech of those people who have any rounding or protrusion at all in their informal speech there is very often some residue of the pouting in /ʃ, ʒ, tʃ, dʒ/ and /r/. Most speakers do retain some pouting and this is a valuable visual clue to this set of consonants.

We have discussed the vowels of English in terms of three parameters—tongue height in mouth (the scale close-open), the backness or frontness of the highest part of the tongue in the mouth (the scale front-back) and the posture of the lips (rounded-unrounded). Two of these variables are much more obvious visually in slow colloquial pronunciation than in informal speech.

There is obviously a necessary relation between tongue height in the mouth and the degree of opening of the jaw. It is impossible, for instance, to articulate a close vowel with the jaw fully open. It is, on the other hand, possible to articulate something that sounds remarkably like an open vowel with the teeth clenched, i.e. with the jaw fully closed. In practice when we teach the English vowels in an idealized pronunciation, we tend to teach close vowels with a nearly closed jaw, and open vowels with an open jaw. Thus we demonstrate the difference in tongue height in the vowels, say of *pea* and *pa* by emphasizing the dimension the student can easily see—the degree of openness of the jaw. In slow colloquial pronunciation it is often possible to observe quite a lot of vertical movement of the jaw. Try saying *see-saws, peacock, knick-knack.* In each case there will be a vertical movement of the jaw downwards into the first vowel, a movement up for the medial consonant and then an even bigger movement downwards for the second level—with a correspondingly bigger movement up to the last consonant. In slow colloquial pronunciation the listener can get a lot of information about which set of vowels a given vowel must belong to simply by watching the degree of opening of the jaw.

We have already observed, in discussing vertical jaw movement for consonants in informal speech, that there is very little vertical movement of the jaw—and if there is none up for the consonant stricture, it must follow that there is none down for the vowel. In most informal speech this is indeed what we find. This means that the foreign student will have to learn to do without the information that vertical movement of the jaw can give him about vowel quality, when he is listening to informal speech.

One of the parameters of vowel description is that which refers to the posture of the lips—whether they are rounded or unrounded. Some English vowels are characterized as being rounded—/ɒ/, /ɔ/, /ʊ/, /u/ and /əʊ/* as in *cot, caught, put, coot* and *coat*, and two become rounded during the articulation of a diphthong—/ju/ as in *new* and /aʊ/ as in *cow*. When these vowels are taught in isolation, the more open vowels—/ɒ/ and /ɔ/—are demonstrated with a slight protrusion of the lips, a curling out, around the wide open mouth, whereas the close vowels /u/ and /ʊ/ are usually demonstrated with tight lip rounding, round a very small central opening.

In informal speech nearly all this lip rounding normally disappears. All the 'rounded' vowels are also back vowels—there is no phonological opposition between back rounded and back unrounded vowels in English, no word shapes are kept apart by this difference—so the rounding feature is, as it were, an extra clue which occurs in slow colloquial pronunciation but does not seem to be necessary in normal informal speech.

It is perhaps rather strong to say that nearly all the lip rounding disappears. The amount of rounding in informal speech varies very much between individual speakers—some appear to have none (and have no rounded or protruded consonants either), others have some rounding and protrusion on some vowels but not on others—those who have rounding and protrusion on vowels in informal speech usually have rounding and protrusion on consonants as well. In all the speakers I have studied there is always more lip protrusion and

---

* The adoption by authors like Gimson of the symbol /əʊ/ in preference to Daniel Jones' /ou/ is of course a recognition of the fact that the phonetic realization of this phoneme is now typically unrounded.

rounding associated with consonants than there is with vowels. The most rounding occurs where consonants which are rounded or protruded in slow colloquial pronunciation occur before stressed vowels which are also rounded or protruded in their slow colloquial form. Thus there is usually rounding and protrusion in words like *rose, shoe, woo* where the same characteristic is shared by both consonant and vowel. On the other hand there may be well be no lip rounding at all in words like *red, ship, will, toes* or *coo*. Similarly in utterances like:

The London stock market was closed this morning.
A spokesman for the Foreign Office denied the charge.

said in informal speech, there will probably be no lip rounding at all. Two of the vowels with rounding—/ɒ/, /ɔɪ/—have very little, if any, pouting out of the lips, even in slow colloquial speech, and this small amount is normally absent from informal speech.

Curiously, those vowels which are often characterized as having close lip rounding—/ʊ/, /u/, /aʊ/ and /əʊ/—seem very likely to lose the rounding in informal speech (except when they are stressed and following a rounded consonant).

The vowel which is most likely to retain lip rounding in informal speech is the vowel in *law* and *caught*, /ɔ/. This is often pronounced, especially when it is stressed, with considerable pushing forward of the corners of the mouth and pouting of the lips round a fairly wide central opening so that the inner, soft part of the lower lip is exposed. The lip rounding is of course even more likely following one of the rounded consonants as in *shore, roar* and *chortle*.

5 The function of intonation

There have been three major traditions in describing the functions of intonation in English. One has largely associated intonation with the expression of attitudes—the 'it's not so much what he said but the way he said it' approach (exemplified, for instance, in O'Connor and Arnold, 1961). One has been largely concerned with relating intonation to syntactic structures (see, for instance Crystal, 1969). The third has been concerned to relate intonation to the speaker's desire to signal to the listener how to treat the information contained in the utterance—a view deriving from work in the Prague School brought to the attention of western scholars most notably by Halliday (see, for instance, Halliday, 1970) and developed recently by Brazil, Coulthard and Johns (1980). I shall leave the discussion of the expression of attitudes until Chapter 6, and concentrate in this chapter on a view which unites the second and third traditions in this sense: it assumes that the speaker does indeed signal to the listener how to take the information contained in the utterance and that one of the relevant forms of such signalling is intonation (together with pause) and that another relevant form of signalling is syntax. It will hardly be surprising, then, that we frequently find intonational and syntactic units have similar domains, since they will be mutually reinforcing.

We should begin the discussion by determining what intonation consists of. I am going to restrict the term to some aspects of variation in pitch of the voice of the speaker and I am going to associate intonation very closely with pause. Other variables—like loudness, tempo, voice quality—I shall call 'paralinguistic features' and discuss separately from intonation in Chapter 6. So in this chapter we are simply going to talk about the organization of the rise and fall in pitch of the voice when the speaker is speaking with 'a straight face', meaning what he says, and is speaking normally loudly, normally fast and within his normal voice range. All of these norms will clearly vary with each individual speaker but, just as with isolated vowels and consonants where we suppose that we can describe, for instance, the articulation of the ideal phonemic /æ/, we must suppose in describing intonation that there is an *unmarked* intonation pattern for any given sentence when it is uttered out of context, in isolation. I shall suppose that this unmarked intonation is most closely represented by the sort of intonation used by a speaker in reading a sentence aloud, out of context and with no indication of any special attitude being given. Consider the following paradigm:

1 'Come with me' he shouted angrily.
2 'Come with me' she said smiling confidently.
3 'Come with me' he ordered.
4 'Come with me' he said.
5 'Come with me' he said invitingly.

It should be clear that, of these, number 4 alone gives no indication of any special attitude on the part of the speaker—all of the others demand some effort of interpretation on the part of the reader, something extra has to be added to mark an order, an invitation, a threat. I shall call the intonation pattern that is not marked by any special attitude an unmarked intonation pattern. All the patterns considered in this chapter are unmarked in this sense. We may continue to draw our examples then from news broadcasts to begin with since one of the characteristics of news broadcasts is that the newsreader speaks in an unemotional way, not expressing any special attitude to what he is reading. Later in the chapter we shall include some examples of discussions arising from news broadcasts in order to move beyond simply reading aloud and to consider the organization of spontaneous speech. Since newsreaders do not utter sentences in isolation the examples of 'isolated sentences' from newsreadings will be of initial sentences in news items—sentences which are not situationally, intonationally, or structurally linked with preceding sentences.

5.1 The 'ideal' organization of tone groups

In all languages speech is organized into stretches of sound continuum with pauses between them. Such stretches are normally co-extensive with a coherent grammatical structure—a phrase, a clause or a sentence. (Occasionally, as we shall see in some examples, we find incoherent chunks of syntax in spontaneous speech, where the speaker is having difficulty in working out what he or she wants to say.) In English such stretches are often patterned intonationally around one dynamic movement of pitch which is more salient than others in the utterance. In speech read aloud it is often easier to identify this salient word (or if the word is polysyllabic, the salient syllable) than it is in spontaneous speech. In the discussion here I shall assume that the easiest way to recognize one of these stretches of speech is by the pauses which flank it on either side. (For a discussion of differences in pause length, refer back to Chapter 3, where they were identified as the 'comma pause', the 'full-stop pause' and the 'paragraph pause'.) Within each of these stretches, called 'tone groups', the salient word will usually be identified as the last lexical item—that is, the item which carries 'end weight' in the tone group and which one tends to remember best precisely because it is the last meaningful word before the pause.

We shall begin by considering some initial sentences in news items: the reason for choosing these is that they do not rely on any immediately previously mentioned information, though, obviously, they do rely on knowledge of the world in general and, if they refer to some event which has been repetitively mentioned over previous news broadcasts, the newsreader may assume some specific knowledge on the part of his audience. In each case, in the transcription of these utterances, the stressed syllables are underlined and the syllable which bears the most salient pitch movement (which is itself always stressed) is printed in capital letters. We shall call this most salient syllable the *tonic* syllable. 'Comma pauses' are indicated by +.

1 Britain's TRADE balance + was in the RED + by a hundred and ninety three million POUNDS last month.
2 The FOREcasters + say that much of England and Wales will be cloudy and WET.
3 AUtumn + seems to be arriving a little EARly this year + and so the season of FOGS + will soon be WITH us.
4 The BUILding employers + and the Unions + are still MEEting.
5 SHARES + have been FAlling + on the London STOCK market.
6 The Bank of ENGland + is accused of dictating TERMS + to the GOvernment.
7 A new PLAN + to boost British CHEESes + is aNNOUNCED.

In all of the examples, even number 7 which is quite short, the sentence which the newsreader has to read is broken up into a sequence of tone groups. In all cases the movement of the pitch of the voice on the *last* tonic syllable in the sentence is greater than that on the previous tonic syllables in the same sentence. So we might represent the overall pattern of example 5, for instance, in the following way:

SHARES + have been FAlling + on the London STOCK market.

This pitch patterning between the tonic syllables serves to mark the unity of the structure which they together form. If we go on to study the organization of a whole news item we shall find that the final tonic syllable in the complete item is marked by an even bigger pitch movement. So all the tonic syllables of what we might call the 'paratone', after the model of 'paragraph', are grouped together. The function of this patterning is to signal to the listener which tone groups are joined together in some larger structure and where the end of the larger structure comes. The most obvious phonetic cues are the high placing of the onset to the paratone, the brevity of the pauses within it, and the gradual drift down in overall pitch height towards the low ending. In the example which we have just examined, each tone group·contains a phrase: a noun phrase, followed by a verb phrase, followed by a prepositional phrase, the three phrases forming one complete sentence.

Now let us consider on what basis each of these initial sentences is divided up into tone groups. A clear general trend can be observed which is to put the *subject* phrase of the sentence into a tone group by itself—all the examples demonstrate this tendency. Examples 4 and 7 which have particularly long subject phrases, divide up the phrase into two tone groups. In 4, each co-ordinate subject phrase has its own tone group, with the *and* being attached, reasonably enough, to the second one. In 7 the subject, *a new plan*, is in one tone group, and the description of the plan, *to boost British cheeses* is in the second.

The next tendency that we can observe is to put the predicate phrase of the sentence into one tone group unless the phrase is particularly long, in which case the predicate may be divided into two tone groups. So in example 1 the long predicate phrase is divided into two tone groups, the first one giving the general information *was in the red* and the second further specifying the information *by a hundred and ninety three million pounds last month*. In 2 despite the very long predicate phrase, containing a second sentence, all the predicate phrase is in one tone group. (It may be that this is particularly true of weather-forecasting style. The weather forecast typically appears at the end of the news bulletin and has to be squeezed into the remaining seconds allowed for the news bulletin.)

In 3 in each of the conjoined sentences the subject-predicate division is made. In 4 and 7 the predicate phrase is in one tone group but in 5 and 6 the long predicate phrase is divided into two tone groups. Again the division of the predicate phrases comes at a natural break—in sentence 5 the second predicate tone group tells us *where* shares have been falling, in sentence 6 the second predicate tone groups tells us *who* it is that the Bank of England is accused of dictating terms to.

It is clear that in general the newsreaders divide the texts which are presented to them on the basis of the *immediate constituent* structure of the sentence. The most likely break is between the two major constituents of the sentence, subject and predicate. The next most likely break will occur within a long subject phrase and/or within a long predicate phrase. This break will also depend on the constituent structure—in each case a clause or phrase which modifies the subject or predicate, gives extra information about them, is likely to be separated off into a tone group of its own.

The most general and important *function* of tone group division then must be seen to be the marking off of coherent syntactic structures which the listener must process as units. It seems clear that there are also other, more specific functions of tone group division which are not entirely understood. Thus in slow formal speech the difference between restrictive and non-restrictive relative clauses may be marked by tone group division:

The boys + who are ill + can't come. (all the boys)
versus
The boys who are ill + can't come. (some of the boys)

It seems likely that this sort of delicate distinction is usually lost in informal speech where, in any case, the situation will usually make it quite clear how the sentence is to be interpreted. Since very few examples of tone groups functioning to disambiguate grammatical structure occurred in the data we shall not consider this sort of function further.

All the tone group divisions in these examples are marked not only by the pitch of the voice falling at the end of each tone group but also by a lengthening of the final syllable of the tone group, so that in this position even an unstressed syllable is longer than it would be elsewhere in the utterance, and also by pauses in the stream of speech. In this particular context then, in the introduction of a new topic by a newsreader reading aloud, we may expect the tone groups to be quite clearly delimited in the stream of speech.

5.2 The 'ideal' placing of the tonic

Now let us turn for the moment from a consideration of tone group divisions (we will return to this in section 5.3) and consider the placing of the *tonic* within each tone group in our examples.

In most of the examples we can see that the tonic syllable falls on the last lexical item in the tone group. This is true of in 1 *red*, in 2 *forecaster, wet*, in 3 *Autumn, fogs*, in 4 *unions, meeting*, in 5 *shares, falling*, in 6 *England, terms, government* and in 7 *plan, cheeses, announced. With*, in the last tone group in 3, must be interpreted as a lexical item, the verb *to be with*. Some apparent exceptions to this general tendency occur in 1 *trade balance*, 4 *building employers* and 5 *stock market*. In each of these the tonic falls on the first item rather than the second. *Trade balance* and *stock market* must be considered to be fixed collocations, compound words in which the tonic is thrown on to the first element just as it is in *blackbird* and *penknife*. *Building employers* is a more complicated case. It is a shorthand term invented by the news media for *employers in the building trade*. From the point of view of news broadcasting *building employers* can also be considered to be a fixed collocation, a compound word. These three compound words may, then, be said to exemplify the general tendency that we have already observed to place the tonic on the last lexical item in the tone group.

The only real exceptions to this tendency are in 1 *last month*, and in 3 *this year*. Time phrases which modify a predicate are very frequently placed last in the tone group and do not receive the tonic—thus *today, yesterday, last year, this week* and *tomorrow* are often found in this position without bearing the tonic. Only if such phrases occur within a context and are used contrastively does the lexical item *year, month, day* acquire the tonic—as in:

The <u>prime</u> <u>mi</u>nister has had to <u>can</u>cel his <u>vi</u>sit to <u>Ply</u>mouth to<u>DAY</u> + but <u>hopes</u> to <u>go</u> to<u>MO</u>rrow

Since we have seen that the major constituents of a sentence—subject and predicate—are assigned to tone groups and that the last lexical item in each tone group is (with a few exceptions) the item within the tone group which is marked as the tonic syllable, we are now in a position to consider the function of the tonic. The function of the tonic is to mark the *centre* or *focus* of the structure of information in any given tone group. We can see the way subsidiary pieces of information group around the head word containing the tonic. In this style of reading aloud the subject word and the main predicate word are clearly marked by the movement of the pitch of the voice on the tonic syllable. Just as foreign students are first taught the slow colloquial, 'idealized' form of words so they should first be taught to recognize the constituent boundaries and the subject-predicate word marking which can be clearly distinguished in a newsreader's rendering of the first introductory sentence of a new news item. And just as advanced students should go on to study how the slow colloquial forms of words in isolation may be modified in informal speech so they should go on to study how tone group boundaries and the whereabouts of the placing of the tonic will be modified when a sentence is used in a given context.

5.3 Tone group and tonic in spontaneous speech

We have considered the initial sentences of texts read aloud by experienced newsreaders—men and women whose ability to communicate the information in the text they are reading is established by the very fact of their continuing employment. I am going to assume that the stress and intonation patterns of these sentences, read before a context is established, represents the 'ideal' use of stress and intonation in speech communication. (There may well be strong theoretical objections to this assumption but I believe it to be an adequate one for our present purposes.) We can summarize this 'ideal' usage in the following way:

(a) *Stress* marks the *lexical words* in the utterance.
(b) *Tone groups* mark off the major constituents of the sentence (subject phrase, predicate phrase, etc.).
(c) *Tonic syllables* mark the last lexical word of the tone group.

Now we shall turn to examine a few short extracts from unscripted radio interviews. In each case the extract is taken from the contribution of an 'expert', usually a politician, an academic or a journalist. Having examined each of them in detail, we shall state general conclusions about their intonational patterning at the end of the section. The reader should bear in mind that these conclusions are only stated for the sort of speech we are examining here—the speech of highly educated men, specialists in their field, who are accustomed to constructing coherent arguments, to 'making speeches'. Presumably this is the type of speaker that the foreign student will be expected to understand in lectures and conferences. The general conclusions may not hold good, though we may expect them to be suggestive, for the less highly structured, spontaneous speech of people less accustomed to making speeches—or indeed to the speech of the same individuals in less public situations.

Extract 1

(Context: why are some groups of immigrants so law-abiding.)

> Because I think they have their OWN + er + very STRONG +
> er + cultural and reLIgious + er + ENtity + + they keep them-
> SELVES + very much to themSELVES + + there may be certain
> dangers in THAT + we're not unduly comPLAcent.

COMMENT

All but the most fluent speakers will have some hesitation markers
in spontaneous speech. These may either be 'filled' pauses where
the speaker utters a schwa vowel (here written as *er*) or unfilled
pauses where there is simply a break in the stream of speech, a short
'comma' pause which is transcribed here as +. A longer pause is
transcribed ++. The pauses mark the break between two tone
groups. Now in the 'ideal' sentences, where the reader was reading
from a prepared text, these pauses came, as we saw, at natural constituent breaks in the sentence. In extract 1 it is clear that the speaker
is thinking what he is going to say next as he goes along. To begin
with, as he marshals his ideas he has the string of not highly information bearing words *because I think they have their own* which leaves
him with a very wide set of options on what to say next. We might
regard this string as a placeholder while the speaker thinks. It is
fluent and uninterrupted and comes out in a very smooth intonation
contour with no break for *I think* which we might have expected to
be marked as an interpolation: *Because + I think + they have their own*
. . . . Then there is a pause while the speaker selects *very strong*
and then another pause while he selects *cultural and religious* and then
finally, rather unexpectedly, he comes up with *entity*. He then glosses
or explains *entity* with a common idiomatic phrase which always has
the tonic placing on the second *themSELVES* and if the phrase is
broken in two, on the first *themSELVES* as well. This completely
automatic phrase *they keep themselves very much to themselves* gives the
speaker time to organize his later remarks, and following it fluently
we find two short sentences each contained in one tone group.

Now compare this extract with the usage we observed in the 'ideal'
sentences:

(a) Stress still marks lexical words in the utterance—every lexical
word is stressed. There are also non-lexical words which are
stressed. These are stressed, I think, for different reasons.
Because is stressed for a stylistic reason. The speaker is speak-

ing slowly at this point, thinking what he is going to say, and instead of saying *because* and following this with a pause he lengthens and stresses the second syllable of *because.*

Own is stressed, and indeed bears the tonic—again because it is being used as a 'pausing' device while the speaker is considering just what he is going to say next, while he selects the next lexical word.

Much is stressed to bring out its intensifying force, *may* is stressed to bring out its limiting force and *not,* again, to bring out its limiting force. All these three could have been pronounced unstressed, with no great change in the meaning of the utterance— stressing them is simply an *intensificatory* gesture. It is possibly relevant to remark that by the second sentence in the utterance the speaker is establishing his, rather slow, rhythm. Stressing these words helps to maintain a basically TUM ti or TUM ti ti rhythm

That is stressed and receives the tonic because it is being used in a deictic way. We might write a decontextualized and explicit form of this sentence in the following way: *There may be certain dangers in their keeping themselves to themselves as opposed to their adopting some other form of behaviour.*

We may make the general observation that a final non-lexical word will only be stressed and receive the tonic when it is either a tonic in an incomplete sentence and being used as a 'hesitation' word or when it is being used contrastively. In the latter case, of course, the tone group in which it occurs will be uttered in some specific context.

(b) Tone groups no longer clearly mark off the major constituents of the sentence. Spontaneous speech is very much less *structured* in this sense than speech where the speaker is reading from a prepared text. Tone groups do, however, in the latter part of this utterance, mark off sentences. So we can see that there is a *tendency,* in spontaneous speech, for tone groups to mark some syntactically cohesive structure of the size of a sentence or less.

(c) We have already mentioned in discussing stress placement that the tonic can occur, in certain circumstances, on non-lexical items. In the first sentence the biggest pitch movement is certainly that on *entity*—to this extent the size of the pitch movements on the tonic syllable marks the end of the 'paratone'.

Extract 2

(Context: employers' representative discussing a union wage claim.)

<u>If</u> there is a <u>certain</u> degree of flexiBIlity + on THEIR side + as <u>well</u> as OURS + there <u>is</u> as I <u>say</u> always HOPE that a <u>set</u>-tlement <u>might</u> eMERGE.

COMMENT

(a) Stress marks all lexical items. Stress also marks some non-lexical items. *If, certain, well, is* and *might* are all examples of words which could be unstressed without materially affecting the meaning of the message. They are examples of what I choose to call 'stylistic' or 'intensificatory' stressing. *Their* and *ours* are not only stressed but also bear the tonic because they are being used contrastively.

(b) The pauses between tone groups mark constituent divisions reasonably clearly up to *there is . . . As I say*, which we might have expected to be marked as inserted just like *I think* in ex-tract 1, is included in the intonation curve of the tone group it appears in. It seems reasonable to assume that very often such insertions have no particular function other than to act as a sort of lexicalized 'filled pause'—giving the speaker the chance to sort out the next thing he is going to say while keep-ing his stream of speech going with a fixed phrase that he does not have consciously to think about.

There is no perceptible break between the two tone groups in the latter half of the sentence. *That a* carries on from the end of the fall in *hope* and leads up to the higher pitch of stressed *settlement*. It seems reasonable to suggest that there might in an 'ideal' reading have been a pause after *hope*.

(c) The tonic always occurs on the last lexical item in the tone group, the head word of the subject phrase or predicate phrase, except in the tone groups where *their* side is contrasted with *ours*. Here the two contrastive items *their* and *ours* bear the tonic.

Extract 3

(Context: on sports training in schools in Britain.)

I THINK + the <u>problem</u> <u>arises</u> when <u>children</u> LEAVE school + + they al<u>ready</u> have deVEloped <u>some</u> poTENtial + and they don't have the opportunity THEN + to go ON with the KIND of + er + SPORT which SHOULD last them for the next ten YEARS.

COMMENT

(a) All lexical items are marked by stress. There are several instances of 'stylistic', 'intensificatory' stressing: *some, don't, should. Then* is stressed and bears the tonic because it is used contrastively: *then—when they leave school* being implicitly contrasted with *while they are at school.*

(b) Tone group divisions begin by marking coherent syntactic units but from *to go on*, apart from the hesitation *er* there is no clearly marked division between tone groups.

(c) The tonic is placed on the last lexical item in each tone group whose boundary is identifiable except in the case of the second tone group—*the problem arises when children LEAVE school.* This is an example of the tonic shifting to the left in the tone group when the last lexical item (or items) has just been mentioned or given or are in some other way given in the context. The context has supplied *in school* and the speaker develops the 'new' topic *leave school.* Since *leave* is new it bears the tonic whereas *school* is merely stressed.

Extract 4

(Context: measures for traffic control on motorways in fog.)

I'm going to introDUCE + mm + as a + certainly as a TRIAL a + a measure of segreGAtion + + this will one cannot make it comPULsory + because of the difficulties of enFORCEment + + but + er + I hope that motorists may feel that it would be SENsible for heavy and light TRAffic + to be segregated in conditions where visibility becomes GREAT and where BRAking + POWer + is + between heavily loaded VEHicles and the LIGHter vehicle is very DIfferent.

COMMENT

This extract may look very unlikely as a piece of dialogue when it is written down in cold print but spontaneous speech of this degree of complexity occurs so frequently in my data that it seemed to me reasonable to consider just one such example. The problem for the foreign student in understanding a sample of speech like that transcribed here is of course, not only one of identifying the words in the acoustic signal, but also of being prepared to discard some of the information and make several hypotheses about what the speaker means to say before arriving at a reasonable hypothesis. As L. R. Palmer (1936, 82) wrote, 'Speech is nothing more than a series of rough hints, which the hearer must interpret in order to arrive at the meaning which the speaker wishes to convey'. Most of the misleading information in the signal occurs in unstressed syllables—*this will, is* but even where a tonic syllable *great* quite clearly contains the wrong lexical item a native speaker will interpret this as some other lexical item that makes sense in the context. He will ignore, or discard, any information which does not positively contribute to the coherent semantic structure which he is trying to compose. One's basic assumption in listening to a speaker is that he intends to say something that makes sense, and one will always tend to interpret anything that he says as something sensible. There are many stories told about this tendency—like that of the man who went round with a happy smile telling people at a party that he had just murdered his wife and the only reaction of his fellow guests was to nod and smile and tell him a funny story. They just did not register what he said because what he said was inappropriate to his expression and the situation. Native speakers of a language have the ability to ignore false starts and hesitations and even tongue slips as gross as that which produces *great* in the extract above. Foreign students have to learn not to stick too closely to the phonetic information but to select and construct from the acoustic signal a reasonable message.

One of the interesting points about this extract is that it gives us an insight into the process by which this speaker composes his message. Since this method of speech composition is at least as common as the method which produces whole, correct, fluent sentences of the sort exemplified in extract 3, we shall pause to consider what we can say about it. The difficulty in producing any extended utterance is that the speaker has to monitor what it is that he has just *finished* saying, while he is producing what he *is* saying at the moment and planning what he is *going* to say in his next sentence. Some speakers manage this enormously complicated process with apparent ease but others, especially those who monitor very critically what it is that they have just said, find the process very difficult, especially in public speaking. Our speaker in extract 4 is clearly one who is very aware of what he has just said and tends to modify it, to improve on it when he realizes that what he has just said will lead him into a difficult piece of syntax or vocabulary. So we find:

as a —certainly as a
this will—one cannot (perhaps avoiding the clumsy 'this will be
difficult to make compulsory')
braking—braking power
braking power is—braking power between . . . is.

On the other hand, one might suggest, he is so busy deciding how
he is going to handle *braking power* when he utters *great* that he does
not register that he has picked the wrong lexical item here.

(a) Once again all lexical items are stressed. Very few non-lexical
items are stressed. *Cannot* and *very* are both 'stylistic',
'intensificatory' stresses, *between* I suspect is stressed because
it was chosen after discarding *is* and the speaker firmly estab-
lishes by stressing it in the item that he has decided to use.

(b) If we ignore the hesitations and false starts we see that the
tone group structuring at the beginning of this extract is more
like our unmarked tone group structuring than that in any
other extract:

I'm going to introduce—certainly as a trial—a measure of
segregation—one cannot make it compulsory—because of the
difficulties of enforcement.

We can guess where the remaining cuts would have come in
an 'ideal' rendering:

I hope that motorists may feel it would be sensible—for heavy
and light traffic—to be segregated in conditions where
visibility becomes great—and where braking power—between
the heavily loaded vehicles—and the lighter vehicles—is very
different.

If this division is plausible the only odd tone group division
that we have to explain is that between *braking* and *power*.
Here, as I have already suggested, we must suppose that the
speaker has changed his mind, decided that *braking* alone was
not sufficiently explicit and added *power*.

(c) If we accept my proposed division of tone groups, in every case
the tonic comes on the last lexical item in the tone group except in the last tone group but one. Here we see again the
movement of the tonic on to the next lexical item to the left
when the last lexical item is *given*. Here *vehicles* is already given
so the tonic moves back on to *lighter*.

One interesting area of investigation that comparison of these, and other, extracts suggests, is to see whether in general when a speaker is highly conscious of the speech he produces and constantly modifies it, he in fact arrives at tone group-tonic-and-stress placement which are more like 'ideal' forms than the placements achieved by more fluent speakers. It would also be interesting to know whether in general the utterances of fluent speakers as against those of 'false start' speakers are more readily understood. One would guess that over short stretches of speech the fluent speaker would be easier to understand. If it were to turn out that 'false start' speakers use less 'stylistic' stressing than fluent speakers, and fewer hesitation phrases like *I think*, it may be that the communicatory efficiency of the 'false start' speaker is at least as great as that of the 'fluent' speaker.

It is clear that the organization of spontaneous speech has much in common with that of 'ideal' sentences read by a competent reader before any context has been established. Stress is consistently used to mark lexical words. It is also occasionally (but relatively infrequently) used to emphasize non-lexical words for what I have called 'stylistic' or 'intensificatory' purposes. Tone group divisions are often less clearly marked in spontaneous speech than they are in 'ideal' speech. Sometimes they are clearly marked by a pause in the stream of speech and lengthening of the final syllable. Sometimes the boundary has to be assumed to follow a tonic bearing item (or the phrase of which the tonic bearing item is the head word). Tone group divisions in spontaneous speech do not mark off subject phrases from predicate phrases as clearly as they do in 'ideal' renderings of written text. This is of course partly a function of the fact that my extracts are drawn from 'comment' programmes or interviews where the interviewee is stating his opinion or intention. It remains true to say that it is clear that the tone groups do in general function to delimit major syntactic constituents.

Similarly just as in the 'ideal' sentences the tonic nearly always marked the head word of the subject or predicate phrase, so in the examples of spontaneous speech the tonic marks the head word of the constituent contained in the tone group. The only regular occasions when the tonic did not occur on the last lexical item were:

(a) when the last lexical item was 'given' in the situation and the tonic moved to the next lexical item to the left,
(b) when the tonic occurred on a non-lexical item which was being *contrasted* with something else.

These two departures from the tonic placing in 'ideal' renderings of sentences are, of course, not only to be found in spontaneous speech but are just as likely to be found used in text read aloud once the context has been established. The intonational device of moving the tonic off the last lexical item, for either of the reasons (a) and (b) above, must be regarded as one of the means whereby a text or discourse is shown to be internally cohesive, to 'hang together'. It is, like the syntactic devices of pronominalization and other means of anaphoric reference, used to show the relations holding between utterances.

5.4 Pitch direction

The aspect of intonation which has traditionally been, and is still, most extensively studied is that of the perceived variation in pitch level, particularly in the pitch patterns on the tonic word and what follows it in the same tone group. The difficulty which faces anyone working on this aspect of intonation is deciding what, from the mass of phonetic data, constitute regular and systematic patterns. It is like the problem which confronts the phonologist when trying to make a phonemic transcription of normal informal speech—how is the phonetic realization which contains 'distorted' (assimilated) or even missing segments, or parts of segments distributed over neighbouring sounds (as when a nasal is realized by nasalization on the preceding vowel) to be related to the 'ideal' structure of the word intended by the speaker? The student of intonation has an even more difficult task than the segmental phonologist because there are many models of English intonation and they bear rather little resemblance to each other: at least phonologists tend to agree on what a phonemic representation of an ideally pronounced word should look like. Phonologists concerned to describe intonation may describe it in terms of a number of pitch levels (which sometimes assimilate to form contours) or a number of basic contours. If they choose a number of basic contours, that number may range from a large number, through smaller numbers like seven, five, three down to two—two is probably the most common.

Let us consider some data (though I should point out that I am not actually offering you 'data' but my transcription, that is, my analysis, of data). Once again I shall assume that the 'ideal' tone patterns are used by newsreaders reading the first, uncontextualized, sentence of a news item. This assumption can, I think, be justified in the description of 'academic' speech which is primarily concerned with the communication of 'intellectual' facts within the framework of a coherent structure of discourse. It would certainly be much less appropriate in the description of 'conversational' speech. The reader should note at this point that the stress and intonational devices which we have considered so far are common to all native accents of English no matter where in the world they are spoken. All native speakers of English stress lexical items, divide their utterance into tone groups marking syntactic units, and mark the head word in the tone group by the tonic. *Tone* on the other hand varies very much between accents, very markedly so even within the accents spoken in Britain, and, within accents, varies to some extent with the individual. It is a curious and surprising fact that it is this highly variable intonational factor which has received so much attention, at the expense of the comparatively stable factors which we have examined in the previous sections.

Extract 1

There's been a <u>sharp</u> re<u>ac</u>tion in the <u>CI</u>ty +

to the <u>Bank</u> of <u>Eng</u>land's <u>WAR</u>nings +

about the <u>danger</u> of in<u>FLA</u>tion + +

COMMENT

The three tone groups here share a very similar tonal pattern. The unstressed syllables at the beginning of the tone group are uttered on a mid-low tone. With the first stressed syllable in each case—*sharp*, *Bank* and *dan(ger)*—the tone jumps sharply to fairly high in the voice range. There is then a gradual descent through unstressed and stressed syllables until the tonic syllable when the pitch of the voice rises at the beginning of the tonic and either falls sharply to fairly low on the next syllable when there is a medial voiceless consonant as in the case of *city* and *inflation* or falls gradually to fairly low when the tonic word is fully voiced as it is in *warning*. The amount of movement from fairly high to fairly low is most marked on the final tonic, *inflation*.

Extract 2

Europe's fiNANCE ministers

meeting in ROME

have agreed on a MAjor step

towards stabilizing CUrrencies

COMMENT

This extract shows more tonal variety. In the first three tone groups the stressed and unstressed syllable before the tonic are all on a fairly even low-mid tone. In the first two tonics the tone moves up on the tonic. The tone continues to move up on *ministers* in the first tone group and at the end of *ministers* has reached about the same height as it does in the curve on *Rome* in the second tone group. In the third tone group the tone moves up at the beginning of *major* and falls through *major* and on through *step*. In the fourth tone group the tone starts from high on the first stressed syllable and steps down through *stabilizing*, starts high again and falls on *currencies*. Again the most marked tonal movement occurs on the tonic of the last tone group, *currencies.*

We may note in passing here that in the first tone group the tonic comes on the second syllable of *finance.* This is, like the pattern *BUILDing employers* that we discussed before, a news media contraction for *ministers of Finance.* This may also be regarded as a fixed collocation or compound in this context. In the third tone group the tonic comes on *major* not on *step.* I do not think that this usage can be attributed to one single factor. I think that it is a combination of the fact that in this context *major* may be held to bear more information than the metaphorical word *step* and the fact that *step* is a very short word—if it were replaced by *movement* or some other two-syllabled word the tonic would be less likely to be on *major.*

Extract 3

In DERbyshire

an R.A.F. Provost JET

CRASHED this morning

on the Derby to Sheffield RAILway line

at UPton

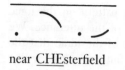

near CHEsterfield

and <u>burst</u> into <u>FLAMES</u>
(The pilot escaped with minor injuries.)

COMMENT

This newsreader is particularly fond of the falling-rising pattern on non-final tone groups. When the tonic comes before the final syllable in the tone group he places a fall on the tonic syllable and then rises through the following syllables. In the second, third, and the last tone groups he uses the pattern we have already met, with a stepping down from a fairly high tone on the first stressed syllable and then the pitch leaps up for a fall on the tonic syllable. The fall then continues through any remaining syllables in the tone group.

The three main tone group patterns that we have observed here are by far the most frequent in all the news items in my data—not only for the initial sentences of an item but for the remaining sentences as well. We may summarize the generalizations thus:

(a) the final tone group always contains a falling tone on the tonic syllable (and on any following syllables, which continue the pattern established in the tonic syllable)

(b) a non-final tone group may either have a falling tonic (which will not fall as far as the final tonic) or a rising tonic, rising to mid-high in the voice range as we saw in extract 2 (again any following syllables continue the pattern established in the tonic) or, finally, there may be a falling tone on the tonic syllable followed by a rise on the following syllables (again rising to mid-high in the voice range)

(c) the first stressed syllable and any following (stressed or unstressed) syllables before the tonic syllable constitute the *pretonic*. The pretonic is either fairly low and level or begins on a fairly high pitch and steps down to fairly low before the tonic syllable. Any unstressed syllables preceding the pretonic will be on a mid-low pitch.

It is not clear that one can say that the pitch pattern on the tonic syllable contributes in any way to the *meaning* of the utterance. We have already seen in discussing the placement of the tonic that the *fact* of the placement of the tonic is significant but it is not clear that which *tone* is selected for the tonic is significant in this kind of speech. There is obviously a general tendency for any tonic that is not final in the sentence not to be realized with a final fall. We might relate this to the very general instruction to children in reading aloud to 'keep your voice up at commas'—that is, do not let the voice pitch fall so far down that you indicate that the end of the sentence has been reached. The stylistic variables for realizing this instruction in newsreading appear to be falling to not-very-low, falling and rising to mid-high or rising to mid-high. The most that we can claim for the 'meaning' of one tone as against another is that it indicates whether a tone group is the final tone group in a sentence or not. Now we shall consider some examples of spontaneous speech.

Extract 4

(Context: location of an Army base)

we have + a BASE + in

what is desCRIBED + _as_ + the + ([ði])

Broadway WORKS + which + is

I think an OLD mill +

on the <u>sou</u> + <u>south</u> <u>west</u> +

<u>COR</u>ner of the +

hospital <u>GROUNDS</u>

COMMENT

This is an example of very careful, deliberate speech with several stressed forms which we might have expected to occur as 'weak forms'. In so far as we can perceive its structuring, it is clear that everything here can be analysed in the terms that we have developed for discussing 'ideal' tone patterns. All the tonics are falls, except for the fall-rise on *old mill*, and the final tonic falls more than the non-final tonics. The pretonics all step down from a high stressed syllable—*Broad(way)*, *think* and *hospital*. We might guess that *south west* really constitutes a similar stepping down before the tonic *corn(er)*. Since it is separated by a pause in the stream of speech I have separated it in the transcription.

Extract 5

(Context: a deposed cabinet minister and his future rôle)

I <u>think</u> he <u>is</u> going to be<u>COME</u> + er + ([gɜn])

an influ<u>en</u>tial <u>FI</u>gure +

but <u>not</u> a figure of any <u>great</u> <u>POWER</u> ([pɑ])

COMMENT

This extract also exhibits the now familiar pretonic which steps down from the first stressed syllable until just before the tonic syllables. All the tonic syllables are falls, the last one being the biggest fall.

Extract 6

(Context: a synthetic meat coming on the market made of ground peas)

In its + <u>MEAT</u> form +

it <u>comes</u> in <u>CHUNKS</u> <u>rather</u> like <u>chuck</u> <u>STEAK</u> +

or <u>MINCE</u> + <u>type</u> <u>FORM</u> <u>si</u>milar to + the + wə + wə + (['səmlətʰ + ð + wə + w])*

you <u>buy</u> <u>MINCE</u> in the <u>BU</u>tcher's

---

* Of course a syllable [w] should be symbolized with a syllabic symbol like [u] but I want to show here that it is the same gesture that the speaker is repeating and prolonging.

COMMENT

The speaker in this extract began confidently but having interrupted the flow with *mince + type form,* took several syllables to recover. This happens quite often in the data.

We have only one new occurrence here—the fall-rise on one syllable in *steak.* Apart from this we have falling tonics on *chunks, mince, mince* and *butcher's* and a fall-rise on *meat form.* There is a pretonic stepping down from stressed *comes* and a level pretonic from *rather.*

I have by no means exhausted the patterning of tones in the data which I have examined. It is true to say, however, that those which I have described are by far the most common in reading aloud and in extended turns. Here there seems to be a fundamental two-way contrast where the essential distinction is between pre-final tones which are *not-low* endings (where the *not-low* ending may be reached either by a fall to mid in the voice range or by a rise) and final tones which are *low* endings and regularly involve a fall to low.

If these are the most common tones in reading aloud and in extended turns (that is, where one speaker speaks for quite a while, perhaps even for as much as an hour, in a lecture), where do the other tones occur? They seem to occur primarily in conversational speech and particularly where speakers contribute very short turns. Thus a reply like *no* or *yes* can be uttered in a multitude of ways, as is suggested by:

'No' she said wonderingly.
'No?' she queried, surprised.
'No' she reflected sadly.
'No' she said determinedly.
'No-o' she said, unable to make up her mind.

It is difficult to give a conclusive account of this variation, which is certainly very extensive and employed by some speakers much more than by others (and by speakers of some accents much more than by others: it seems, for instance to be much more common among southern English RP speakers than among speakers of Scottish English). These tonal 'wiggles', rise-falls, fall-rises, fall-rise-falls, etc., seem to have a primarily stylistic modal function which is sometimes intensificatory, and sometimes modifies the effect of the utterance as in *no-o.* They frequently occur together with the forms of paralinguistic variable which we shall discuss in the next chapter. These 'stylistic wiggles' seem to me to be appropriately regarded as decorations, which are, by some speakers, in some circumstances, added to the basic tonal structure of English which, as I have suggested, can be reduced to the low/not-low distinction.

6 Paralinguistic features

Paralinguistic features of speech are those which contribute to the expression of attitude by a speaker. They are phonetic features of speech which do not form an intrinsic part of the phonological contrasts which make up the verbal message: they can be discussed independently of the sequences of vowels and consonants, of the stress patterns of words, of the stressing of lexical rather than grammatical words, and of intonation structure which determines where the tonic syllable falls. Hitherto the features of speech which we have discussed have been features which contribute directly to the interpretation of the verbal content of the message and its organization by the speaker in terms of information structure. Now we turn to consider those aspects of speech which contribute to a meaning over and above what the verbal element of the message means. Following a well-established distinction, we shall call the meaning contributed by the verbal content the 'conceptual' meaning of the utterance, and the meaning contributed by the paralinguistic features the 'affective' meaning of the utterance, where the feelings and attitudes of the speaker are to some extent revealed to the listener. (For a fuller discussion of this distinction, see Leech, 1974.)

The paralinguistic features of speech are not, of course, isolated from other modes which are available to the speaker by which a particular attitude can be indicated towards the person being addressed or towards what is being spoken of. They relate closely to the phenomenon often referred to as 'body talk' or 'body language'—which refers to gesture, posture, facial expression and so on, all of which may have an effect on the way the listener interprets what the speaker says. If the speaker says 'That's very interesting' leaning forward with a bright alert look, the listener is likely to think that this is really what the speaker means, whereas if the speaker utters the same words but twisting to look out of the window and stifling a yawn, the listener might reasonably conclude that the speaker is not actually very interested. The body language of the speaker forms part of the wider context of utterance in which what is said is interpreted. I shall concentrate on the paralinguistic features of speech, rather than include a general discussion of these features within the wider setting of body language in general, because these are features which we listen to, and which we can hear over the radio, telephone or tape recorder—they fall squarely within the province of a discussion of 'listening' to spoken English. In our everyday experience of language it is usually the case that the paralinguistic vocal features will reinforce the content of what the speaker says. Thus our unmarked, neutral expectation will be that someone who says 'What a lovely day' will say it enthusiastically, that someone who says 'I am sorry' will say it sincerely, and that someone who says 'And now get out of here' will say it angrily. It is relatively rare, but by no means uncommon, to encounter a mismatch between the verbal content of the utterance and the way it is said—it is on such occasions that expressions like 'It's not so much what he said as the way he said it that upset/struck/infuriated me' are appropriately used. Where such a mismatch occurs, listeners tend to pay more attention to the way something is said than to the verbal content. Lyons (1972) writes of this phenomenon in the following terms:

> It seems to be the case that, whenever there is a contradiction between the overt form of a verbal utterance and the associated prosodic and paralinguistic features it is the latter which determine the semiotic classification of the utterance.

Imagine how you would react if a friend came into the room where you were and said cheerfully 'I have just failed my exam'. It would not be appropriate for you to put on a grave face and sympathize, as you probably would have, if she had been depressed at the news. You are very much more likely to ask her why she wanted to fail her exam, or why she thinks it is amusing, than to express sympathy. A mismatch between the content of the utterance and the paralinguistic features is sometimes interpreted as 'ironic': thus if a boring anecdote is told and then one of the listeners says, in a dead-pan voice with no indication of amusement 'very funny', he may be accused of irony (or indeed of sarcasm, the two are rarely consistently distinguished in modern English).

The problem of discussing paralinguistic vocal features is that there is no generally agreed accessible framework of description which is known to the general reader, since there is no long tradition of description in this area, unlike those aspects which we have discussed in earlier chapters where there is an extensive tradition of description to call upon. (For modern descriptions see, for example,

Crystal, 1976, Laver 1980.) Some of the features which I shall list are, I believe, perfectly accessible; others will require careful exemplification in order to remind you of your own previous experience of the feature I have in mind. The best hope of securing examples where you and I are likely to share a similar consciousness of how the words would be uttered seems to me to lie in quotations from conversation in literary works. An author who wishes to show that a character is speaking in a certain manner assumes that it is possible so to describe the manner of speaking that the reader has a good idea of how it should sound. The fact that authors do this, that readers habitually cope with it, and that readers-aloud often adopt the same sorts of paralinguistic features to express a given emotion or attitude, suggests that there are regular, conventional, relationships between some descriptive terms and the paralinguistic features which they evoke. Authors rely on these conventional relationships to describe the manner in which words are uttered so as to reinforce the content or to contradict the meaning of the uttered words.

Here are some examples of 'reinforcement' from E. M. Forster's *Howards End*:

'But you will be careful, won't you?' she exhorted. (55)
'Of course I don't mind,' said Helen, a little crossly. (56)
'Oh, hush!' breathed Margaret. (57)
'Bother the whole family!' snapped Margaret. (62)

In each case the author tells us how the utterance is to be spoken and in each case the description is one which tallies very well with what is being expressed. It is comparatively rare in literature as in life to find examples where the description of how the utterance to be spoken suggests a different attitude on the part of the speaker from what his words, taken at their face value, suggest. Here are some examples of this from that master of subtlety, Henry James, from *Portrait of a Lady*:

'Yes, I'm wretched,' she said very mildly. (488)
'*Do* you know I love you?' the young man said, jocosely, to Isabel a little later, while he brushed his hat. (32)
'I'm sure I don't care whether you do or not!' exclaimed the girl; whose voice and smile, however, were less haughty than her words. (32)

All of the features we shall discuss here are *relative* features. For example: individual A normally speaks loudly, and individual B normally speaks very quietly. Suppose they both deviate from their accustomed amplitude and speak more loudly than usual. We may write "'Go away" said A loudly', and "'Go away" said B loudly'. A's *loudly* may well be more loud than B's. B's *loudly* may be no louder than A's normal speech but, since it represents a departure from normal, it may be described as *loud.* Similarly A may normally speak quite fast, and B quite slowly. If we write A or B spoke *hurriedly* it simply indicates a departure from the normal habit of the individual, not from some abstract, absolute norm.

In fact it seems very likely that each society has some notion of an abstract norm of speech. The fact that different members of society agree that A speaks loudly, or rapidly, or gruffly, indicates that there is some norm, however ill defined, by which individuals are judged. Indeed it seems likely that we judge people's characters to some extent by how they relate to this norm. We think of someone who habitually speaks rapidly, breathily and with a lot of movement up and down in her voice range as 'excitable', of someone who habitually speaks in a very quite voice, with very little pitch movement, as 'withdrawn'. I am not concerned here with the permanent features of an individual which constitute his personal norm. I am concerned with the patterns of variation from the norm which are interpreted by listeners as modifying a given utterance.

6.1 Pitch span

Each individual has a part of his voice range within which he normally speaks. With some individuals the range is quite wide and with others quite narrow. There is always some voice range above the normal speech range, what we might call the 'squeak' range, and some voice range below, what we might call the 'growl' range, which is not used at all in 'unmarked' speech. We can represent it like this:

'squeak' range
normal speaking range
'growl' range

All the examples in Chapter 5 were written between just two lines. They were spoken within the normal speaking range of the individual. When I spoke of 'mid-high', 'mid-low', 'low' and so on I was always referring to some point within the normal speaking range—not within the total available voice range of the individual. If you refer back to the diagrams representing intonation patterns in the last chapter you will see that the pitch of the voice did not at any point reach near the top of the normal speaking range, though in final falls the end of the fall was fairly near the bottom of the normal speaking range. This final fall has about the same amount of pitch movement or span as a word spoken in isolation. In order to keep the picture as simple as possible we shall examine, to begin with, one word utterances and we shall consider the neutral word *hallo* as it might be spoken to indicate different attitudes on the part of the speaker.

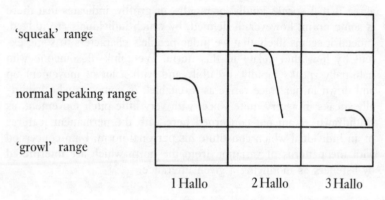

'squeak' range

normal speaking range

'growl' range

1 Hallo   2 Hallo   3 Hallo

At the moment we are only discussing the variable of how much movement in the pitch of the voice there is. Let us contextualize these possible utterances. A meets B in a corridor. In 1 he says *Hallo* starting from mid-high and falling to low, the *mid fall*. This is the 'unmarked', newsreaders' manner of speaking. If a novelist were describing this he would write merely 'John said "Hallo" to Bill as he passed him in the corridor'—there is no particular attitude indicated here.

In 2 however, which starts from high in the normal speaking range, or even in the 'squeak' range some attitude *is* indicated. Quite how we decide to interpret the attitude will depend on other variables. If, for instance, it is said with a smile and a breathy quality in the voice it might be interpreted as *happy* or *excited*. If raised eyebrows and wide open eyes are added it might be *excitedly surprised*. If we take away the smile and the breathy voice and turn down the corners of the mouth it might be *disagreeably surprised*. The point is that a wide span in pitch, when it is a departure from the normal pitch span, indicates that *some* attitude is being expressed. Pitch span alone does not indicate *what* that attitude is. The *high fall* itself is simply an indicator that some positive attitude, some departure from the speaker's normal attitude, is being expressed.

If speaker A meets B in the corridor and addresses him as in our second example with a big falling *Hallo* he will be hurt and surprised if B does not respond in any way, or if B simply says *Hallo* with a mid fall as in example 1. A has exposed some attitude, some emotion—he has, as it were, opened himself to the possibility of being rejected. By using this high fall, especially if it is combined with friendly gestures—a smile, a 'warm tone of voice'—he has put himself in a vulnerable situation. The appropriate response of B, unless B is very unfriendly, is to use the same big pitch pattern and, if A is smiling and being friendly, to smile and perhaps even to stop to chat.

If A meets B and utters a *Hallo* on a *low fall* he is declining to expose any positive attitude. It is the very smallest response he can make to B's presence. Again the amount of fall cannot by itself determine what attitude is being expressed. If the *Hallo* is very brief, uttered very quickly with a 'tense' voice quality our novelist might write '"Hallo," John said snappishly'. If on the other hand it is uttered in a whisper he might write, '"Hallo," John said in an undertone', or 'conspiratorially'. If it is spoken with the eyes of the speaker turned away from B and the lips slightly pursed '"Hallo," said John coldly'. What the narrowness of pitch span appears to indicate is the refusal to express any emotion which renders the speaker vulnerable in the way that using the high fall does. A will not be unduly hurt if B does not respond to him—he is certainly not inviting him to stop and chat.

Obviously there is more to pitch span variation than simply three possibilities but from a teaching point of view these three certainly form a reasonable basis for discussion.

They can be summarized thus:

$$\text{pitch span} \begin{cases} 1 & \text{medium span —unmarked} \\ 2 & \text{extended span —exposed emotion} \\ 3 & \text{restricted span —exposed emotion} \end{cases}$$

The high fall is regularly associated with *loudness* in my analysis of the examples given here. I think this association is quite common.

Let us turn now to some examples which suggest that a restricted pitch movement is being used:

1 'Here he comes,' she murmured, and they could hear that her lips were dry with emotion.

Tess of the D'Urbevilles (186)

2 'I hope I am not too heavy?' she said timidly.

Tess of the D'Urbevilles (187)

3 'I thought you mightn't stand it.' Her voice was high, steady, uninflected.

Time of Hope (353)

4 'Please, sir, nobody seems to care to come,' she muttered, dully resigned all at once.

Amy Foster (255)

Murmured and *muttered* I think always indicate restricted pitch. In 3 it is specifically stated that the voice is 'uninflected'. 2 is more open to question than the others. *Timid* suggests to me soft, rather than loud, and this is often accompanied by restricted pitch span. (Soft rather than loud is of course also implied by *murmured* and *muttered*.) 2 certainly *could* be spoken with unmarked pitch span.

Here are some examples from novels which suggest to me that extended pitch movement is being used:

1 'His guilt and his descent appear by your account to be the same,' said Elizabeth angrily.

Pride and Prejudice (92)

2 'Really, Mr. Collins,' cried Elizabeth with some warmth, 'you puzzle me exceedingly.'

Pride and Prejudice (106)

3 'But I don't want anybody to kiss me, sir!' she implored, a big tear beginning to roll down her face.

Tess of the D'Urbevilles (66)

4 'I don't know any saints,' she said desperately.

A Burnt Out Case (70)

5 'You're at an ordinary English week-end party, sir,' thundered the Major-General.

England Their England (79)

6 'Consult you!' she exclaimed, scornfully interrupting him. 'I never heard of such a thing! Why should I consult you as to my movements?'

Cashel Byron's Profession (120)

Elizabeth's anger and warmth in examples 1 and 2 both require room in the pitch span for expression. The big pitch movement will also be accompanied by other variables—one would expect that both these sentences would be uttered rapidly rather than slowly, and loudly rather than softly, to mention only two. *Implored* and *desperately* both indicate a stress of uncontrolled emotion which will be realized with a big pitch movement. Again the situation demands a rapid rather than slow speed of delivery and these distraught girls will both speak loudly in order to make their plea more clearly heard. Loudness is a clear accompaniment of the big pitch movement demanded by *thundered* in example 5, though this time a slower pace of delivery seems indicated—it is difficult to imagine something as portentous as *thunder* being uttered rapidly. *Exclaimed* (like *cried*) is a word used very frequently by novelists though it is rarely found in speech—perhaps because it has the sole function of expressing a big pitch movement and, unless this is expressly contradicted in a given example, a rapid utterance. (Notice, incidentally, in example 6, the necessary placing of the tonic on the first *consult* ('conSULT you') and the second *you* ('consult YOU').

6.2 Placing in voice range

Now we shall look to see what the effect is of placing these various pitch spans in different parts of the total voice range. Obviously there are many possibilities but we have space only to examine a few combinations.

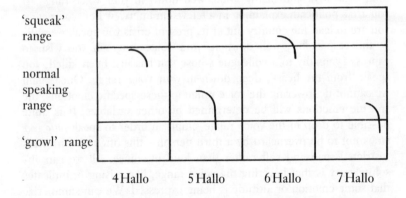

A is still meeting B in the corridor. If A says *Hallo* to B, with a very restricted pitch span high up in his normal speaking range B might conclude that A was either in some withdrawn state or was afraid of him—certainly that he was in a *nervous* state of some sort. It is a very common experience that when we are nervous our voices shoot up in the voice range—just as the rest of the bodily musculature contracts under nervous tension, so do the muscles controlling the glottis and its position in the throat.

Example 5 is an example of a very restricted use of *Hallo*—used exclusively, I believe, by a member of the male sex towards a young and pretty member of the female sex. It finishes well down in the masculine 'growl' range.

If the normal, unmarked span is lifted into the top of the normal speaking range, even partly into the 'squeak' range this seems often to correlate with a state of nervousness or excitement (but without the fear of showing any emotion that we see in the restricted span of 4). Again the mere fact of lifting the span does not explicitly specify the emotion—other variables will pin that down. What the raising *does* is indicate that some positive attitude or emotion is being expressed.

If the normal unmarked span is lowered into the lower part of the normal speaking range, or even into the 'growl' range, this very frequently appears to correlate with the desire to express involvement, sincerity, responsibility, heartfelt emotion, dedication and so on. Certainly if one wants to express any of those emotions or attitudes one will go well down in one's normal speaking range to do it. If you are a young man anxious to convince Mr Smith that you really are able to offer a respectable prospect to his daughter, or work hard in his firm, or sell his product well, you try to say this with conviction, in a 'firm and manly' tone, well down in your voice range. If you are a politician explaining in a television interview how competent you are to lead the country out of its present crisis you speak weightily and responsibly, well down in your voice range. If you wish to express sympathy to a colleague whose son has just been killed, you speak 'from the heart', deep down in your voice range. Once again we cannot tie lowering the voice range to these specific emotions, the specific emotions will be determined by other variables. It is quite possible to drop in the voice range simply in order to speak *sotto voce* so as not to be overheard by a third person—this often also involves restricted span and soft rather than loud utterance. All we can absolutely say is that lowering the voice range, like raising it, indicates that some emotion or attitude is being expressed. We can summarize this in a rather inconclusive way, like this:

placing in   { 1 middle placing   —unmarked
voice range   { 2 raised or lowered placing—attitude/emotion

Here are some examples which suggest that the top of the voice range is used:

1 'This!' shrieked the miserable man. 'I never heard of it!'
The Wrong Box (83)

2 'Leave me alone—damn you. I am all right,' screeched Jukes.

Typhoon (208)

3 Greggie continued to shrill at Mrs Dobell above the clamour of the girls, the street-crowd, the ambulances, and the fire-engines. 'It was ten chances to one we might have been in the garden when the bomb went off .... We would have been buried, dead, killed. It was ten to one, Mrs Dobell.'

The Girls of Slender Means (115)

All the *scream, shriek, screech, shrill* words suggest a raised placing in the voice range. Extract 3 in the last but one set of examples also suggested raised placing—'her voice was high, steady, uninflected'. That example, together with the three I have just quoted, are all describing the speech of people at the end of their emotional tether. They all suggest loud and rapid utterance.

All the examples of extended pitch span in 6.1 also suggest extension into the high voice range. The *muttered* and *murmured* examples that we have already considered suggest lowered placing in the voice range as well as restricted pitch span. Other examples suggesting lowering in the pitch range are:

1 'You were expecting more?' purred the siren admiringly.

England Their England (64)

2 'I hope you're right,' said the Major-General gloomily.

England Their England (75)

3 'And now, sir,' she added earnestly, 'can you tell me this—will it be just the same for him as if you had baptized him?'

Tess of the D'Urbevilles (123)

4 'You shall not speak to Miss Hazeltine in that way,' said Gideon sternly.

The Wrong Box (83)

Purred has a very precise meaning and indicates not only lowering in the voice range but soft rather than loud speech, slow rather than rapid. *Gloomily* and allied words—*disappointed, depressed, miserably, grumpily*—indicate lowered placing in the voice range. *Gloomily* also suggests slow rather than rapid speech and a pitch span that is certainly not extended (that would show too much animation) and may well be reduced. *Earnestly* and associated words—*seriously, gravely, soberly*—indicate a drop into the 'responsible' voice range that I have already discussed. They also suggest slow rather than rapid delivery and unmarked or extended, rather than reduced, pitch span. *Sternly*, and other words indicating displeasure being expressed by someone with the power to recriminate, also drop into the 'responsible' pitch range.

6.3 Direction of pitch

The 'unmarked' direction of pitch in English is the *fall*. The *high rise*—the rise from fairly low in the voice range to high, even into the 'squeak' range occurs only rarely in my news broadcasting and discussion data. It occurs rarely in recordings I have of spontaneous private conversation and then only when directly querying something that has just been said—either as a simple 'echo' question where the whole of a short preceding sentence is repeated, with the high rise tonic on the tonic syllable:

I saw him on THURSday

You saw him on THURSday

or as a partial 'echo question' where some piece of the previous sentence is repeated with a high rise tonic on the item being questioned:

He can hardly be expected to take action on a problem

that only concerns PETer.

You think it's really a PROBlem?

It also occurs as a question on the whole content of some previous statement where there is no explicit echo—questions of the *Do you really think so?* variety.

The high rise always involves extended pitch span and, in the examples I have cited, expresses some strong reaction to what has just been said—surprise, incredulity, etc. It *challenges* the correctness of what has been said.

It is often suggested in the literature on intonation that the high rise is the normal intonation pattern to find on *yes-no* questions—questions which do not begin with one of the *wh* words (*who, what, why, when, how* etc.). According to this view one would expect to find the high rise on questions like:

1 Do you beLIEVE + that price rises can be curTAILed?

2 And this is going to be put on the MARKet + and

  sold to the PUBlic + IS it?

3 But isn't it a FACT + that the government is going

  to be FORCED + into some sort of STATutory price

  policy + before many weeks or months are OUT?

4 Is it not possible for the army to withDRAW from

  the hospital + and do the same job somewhere ELSE?

5 Could YOU handle it?

On all these questions, and others like them in the broadcast data, the tonic is a *fall* not a high rise. I suspect we need to study the incidence of the high rise in a good deal of detail and over a lot of data in different situations before we make too strong claims for its distribution. In my data, as I have said, it is rare, and nearly always occurs in the questioning of some previous assertion. It does occasionally occur in *yes-no* questions, where, it seems to my subjective judgement, the questioner is either trying to conciliate his interviewee (as in the case of a reporter interviewing some very indignant building workers) or to express respect for his interviewee (as in the case of a reporter interviewing a member of the cabinet). Since these intentions are very similar we could lump them together as 'conciliatory'.

The high rise may not however be confined to 'challenging' or 'conciliatory' attitudes (and note here that these very opposite attitudes will have to be specified by other variables than the high rise). The most we can say, I think, about the high rise in the present state of our knowledge is that, whether respectfully or challengingly or stridently, it *demands a response*. I think that it is unfortunate that it has been linked with the notion of 'questioning' and that statements like *a rising intonation can turn a statement into a question* have been uttered. 'Question' is a very useful formal term for teachers to use in exercises which require students to change statements into questions. There are well-known formal qualities which questions in this sense share—the introduction of a *wh* word or auxiliary verb-subject inversion as in *Is John coming?* Teachers would hardly be pleased to find students simply tacking on question marks to indicate a rising intonation in such an exercise. It quickly becomes obvious that the formally marked sentence is not equivalent in meaning to the intonationally marked question and is not appropriate to the same situation. Consider:

Statement:	The doctor's coming.
Question:	1 Is the doctor coming?
	2 The doctor's coming?

Question 2 can only be uttered as a response to the immediately preceding statement. It does not ask the open question whether or not the doctor is coming, as question 1 does. What it does is query the correctness of the assertion made in the immediately previous statement. It should not be considered as a question equivalent to question 1. (I suspect it would be better to call it by some other name than 'question'.) This is an example of the *challenging* use of the high rise.

The function of pitch direction in conveying attitude must, I think, be restricted to the following statement:

$$\text{pitch direction} \begin{cases} 1 \text{ fall} & \text{—unmarked} \\ 2 \text{ high rise} & \text{—demands a response.} \end{cases}$$

6.4 Tempo

Everyone has a normal tempo of speech. Sometimes a speaker speaks *faster* than at other times. We cannot judge the significance of the change in speed if the change is simply considered as a phenomenon by itself. Speed may be associated with urgency—the delivery of an important message in a hurry. In this case we might expect the speaker to be breathless, to speak in gasps, to simplify segments as much as possible, to speak in a raised voice range. Any sort of pressure of time on a speaker, the possibility of the telephone pips cutting off his call, the possibility of another speaker interrupting him, may cause a speaker to quicken his tempo. He speaks more quickly in order to get all he has to say in a potentially limited amount of time. But rapidity of delivery may not simply indicate actual pressure of time. If speaker A wants to suggest to speaker B that their conversation has lasted quite long enough, and that he has no more time to spend talking to B, he may quicken his speech, even glance at his watch, to suggest that he really must go and get on with all the things he has to do. Here A is using rapid speech as a sort of paralinguistic metaphor—to suggest that he is pressed for time (even though he is not) he quickens his speech.

Rapid speech may arise from situations that have nothing to do with pressure of time or desire to invoke pressure of time. For example if A has some distasteful message to convey to B he may wish to 'get it over as quickly as possible'. Just as we found we could not pin pitch variation down to any specific emotion or attitude, so rapidity of speech cannot be pinned down to a single attitude. We will find however that there are some emotions or attitudes that seem to imply rapidity of speech.

Slow tempo cannot be associated with any specific set of attitudes. A speaker may speak slowly simply because he is thinking very carefully about what he is saying. Equally a speaker may speak slowly because he wishes to give the *impression* that he is thinking carefully about what he is saying. Many public figures speak slowly, well down in the voice range, with lots of stressed words, long-drawn-out tonic syllables and significant pauses:

WE + have COME + to a POINT + from which we may NOT + DRAW + BACK.

Speech of this sort may be described by adjectives like *responsible, significant, heroic, ponderous* or *pretentious* according to the taste of the observer. For the moment we shall simply say that for

tempo $\begin{cases} 1 & \text{normal tempo is unmarked} \\ 2 & \textit{rapid or slow} \text{ tempo is marked for attitude.} \end{cases}$

We have already observed many instances when rapidity or slowness of speech seems to co-occur with other variables. Let us however look briefly at one or two examples of slow and rapid speech:

1 I said slowly: 'I think that we must part'.

Time of Hope (344)

2 'The United States Army . . .' began the Major-General with impressive slowness.

England Their England (80)

3 'Miss Spenlow, if you please,' said her father majestically.

David Copperfield (415)

4 'I've been finding things in the Forest,' said Tigger importantly.

The House at Pooh Corner (31)

In 1 the speaker is addressing his wife after long and bitter consideration. He is 'breaking' the news gently to her. Bad news is conventionally 'broken gently', slowly, to the afflicted. The schoolmaster in *David Copperfield* slows him down as he is taken upstairs to be told of his mother's death: "Don't hurry, David,' said Mr Sharp. 'There's time enough, my boy, don't hurry." (92). In 2, 3 and 4 the slowness is combined with a feeling of personal importance and hence the necessary significance of what is being said.

Here are some examples which indicate rapid speech:

1 'But what did he say?' gasped Morris.

The Wrong Box (88)

2 She went on breathlessly: 'Then they are going to run off together!'

Return of the Native (448)

3 'Never mind,' I said crisply, 'I have my methods.'

The Inimitable Jeeves (44)

4 'I dare say I'm unfair. But this is important. There are others who'd do it admirably.' I rapped out several names.

Time of Hope (344)

5 'You're in Ormerode Towers,' snapped Miss Perugia Gaukrodger.

England Their England (79)

In 1 we find another almost exclusively literary term *gasped*. Anyone who *gasps* utters what he is saying on one short tone group—there are also clear indications of 'breathy' voice quality, even *indrawn* breath. The same 'breathy' voice quality is found in 2 where we have an example of a message being delivered in great haste by someone who has run all the way to deliver it. These two are clearly apart from the voice quality indicated by *crisply*, *rapped out* and *snapped*. These last three are all examples of speech being rapid because the speaker is impatient.

6.5 Loudness

Everyone has a normally loud way of talking. To some extent each individual will vary the loudness of his speech with the situation in which he finds himself. If he is speaking in public he will speak more loudly than if he is speaking privately. Within this general variation there are instances where an utterance is spoken loudly or softly and where this departure from the norm has some attitudinal significance. As we have seen, loudness and softness are often closely associated with pitch span. It is difficult to speak loudly on a very restricted pitch span (which is perhaps why the television robots, the Daleks, sound so inhuman). It is rare to find an extended pitch span used while speaking softly. Let us examine some instances of *loud* and *soft* speaking in literature:

1 'The low fiend of Hell!' shouted Mr Huggins indignantly.

England Their England (226)

2 'Do not be afraid of *my* wanting the character,' cried Julia, with angry quickness.

Mansfield Park (104)

3 'Adèle here ran before him with her shuttlecock. 'Away!' he cried harshly; 'keep at a distance, child.'

Jane Eyre (171)

4 'To-morrow? Oh, I should LOVE TO!' she cried. Her voice expanded into large capitals because by a singular chance both the neighbouring orchestras stopped momentarily together, and thus gave her shout a fair field.

Tales of the Five Towns (100)

5 'You were scared weren't you?' she accused him. 'You wanted to live!' She spoke with such force that in his shocked state Dick wondered if he had been frightened for himself.

Tender is the Night (212)

All these examples involve *loud* rather than unmarked or *soft* speech. In each case the character is expressing some strong emotion — in 1 and 2 anger, in 3 irritation, in 4 excitement and in 5 scorn. In the examples here we might also expect rapid rather than slow speech.

Murmured, muttered and *timid* have occurred in previous examples and we noted then that these imply *soft*ness rather than *loud*ness.

1 Izz lowered her voice. 'Marian drinks.'

Tess of the D'Urbevilles (344)

2 'We were unlucky, Miss Price,' he continued in a lower tone, to avoid the possibility of being heard by Edmund.

Mansfield Park (170)

Authors very often indicate confidentiality by having a character lower his voice. *Lowered* his voice seems primarily to suggest reduction in amplitude but it may be that it also indicates lower placing in the voice range.

The effect of *loudness* may be stated thus:

loudness $\begin{cases} 1 \text{ normal} \qquad \text{—unmarked} \\ 2 \text{ loud or soft —some attitude is being expressed.} \end{cases}$

6.6 Voice setting

So far we have considered paralinguistic features which are reasonably familiar—pitch span, placing in voice range, direction of pitch, tempo and loudness. We turn now to discuss the effect of various adjustments in the vocal cords which give rise to different effects of voicing. There are many possible adjustments of the vocal cords but here I am going to discuss only three: the *normal* vocal cord setting of the individual, voicing which is accompanied by breathiness which I shall call 'breathy' and voicing which gives an effect rather like a cat's purr which I shall call 'creaky' voice.

We can indicate the scope of 'breathy' voice by considering some of the descriptive terms that have appeared in our literary quotations: *panted, gasped, whispered, breathed, huskily, breathlessly.* Most of these suggest some seepage of voiceless air accompanying voicing. *Panted,* and *breathlessly* also suggest breathing quickly, and *gasped,* speaking on an indrawn breath. *Whispered* and *breathed* may well suggest no voicing at all but I think are often used simply to suggest *soft* 'breathy' voice. Certainly each term can be further defined but it seems reasonable to suggest that this whole set shares the feature 'breathy' voice. 'Breathy' voice is not, of course, a significant feature if it arises simply because an individual is out of breath. We are only concerned here, as I said in 6.1, with variations from the norm that the listener interprets as modifying the utterance.

'Creaky' voice very often accompanies *lowered* placing in the voice range and is very frequently found in RP in expressing a 'responsible' attitude. It seems always to accompany the expression of deeply-felt sympathy for example. Descriptive terms implying 'creaky' voice are not so obvious as those for 'breathy' voice but I suggest the following: *purred, gratingly, murmured, majestically, earnestly. Purred* and *murmured* are both placed low in the voice range and both imply soft rather than loud, slow rather than rapid speech. *Gratingly* suggests to me loud rather than soft, unmarked for tempo, unmarked for placing in voice range, 'creaky' with *tense* articulatory setting. (We come to articulatory setting in the next section.) *Majestically* and *earnestly* both describe speech placed low in the voice range.

The function of voice setting may be expressed like this:

voice setting $\begin{cases} 1 \text{ normal} & \text{—unmarked} \\ 2 \text{ breathy or creaky—some emotion or attitude} \\ & \text{is being expressed.} \end{cases}$

6.7 Articulatory setting

This is not in some ways a very satisfactory variable because several different phonetic features are involved. What I want to do here is suggest some notion of an overall *tense* setting of the articulatory tract as against an unmarked, normal setting. This 'tenseness' is frequently, but not always, especially marked by the hardening of the musculature in the pharyngeal cavity—the part that is affected when one suffers from a sore throat. It seems reasonable to suggest that this tension of setting is associated with a strongly felt emotion which is often not being fully expressed verbally. Just as I suggested that high placing in the voice range may often be associated with nervous tension so may *tense* articulation be associated with a state of nervous emotion. Here are some extracts where the author seems to me to be suggesting *tense*ness of articulation:

1 'Who rang up?' Donald asked in a voice that was as near a bark as he had ever got in the course of his mild and gentle life.

England Their England (67)

2 'Good-bye,' he replied, through his teeth.

Cashel Byron's Profession (124)

3 He said sharply, 'For God's sake, don't start taking me for an example, too.'

A Burnt Out Case (180)

4 'Don't you see,' she said, with a really horrible bitterness, with a really horrible lamentation in her voice, 'Don't you see that that's the cause of the whole miserable affair; of the whole sorrow of the world?'

The Good Soldier (45)

Other descriptive terms which I think suggest this *tenseness* are: *snapped, rapped, coldly, stiffly, sternly, icily, scorn, frightened, terrified, disdainfully.* We can summarize this as:

articulatory setting $\begin{cases} 1 \text{ normal—unmarked} \\ 2 \text{ tense} \quad \text{—expresses emotion.} \end{cases}$

6.8 Articulatory precision

In Chapter 4, I described typical simplifying patterns that occur in my data. These patterns occur in the speech of most of the speakers I have listened to. There are, however, occasions when a speaker who normally makes these simplifications suddenly does not do it. He speaks slowly and very precisely, releasing final consonants before following initial consonants—as in:

['gʌvɜnmənt^h'waɪt^h'p^{h}eɪpə]   Government white paper

and uttering some (but not all) of the grammatical items he uses in their 'strong' rather than 'weak' forms:

[ðɪ + 'əʊnlɪp^{h}ɒsɪ'bɪlɪtɪ + ɪz + ðə'wʌnaɪhævsʌ'dʒestɪd]
The only possibility is the one I have suggested

The effect of this sudden articulatory precision is that the speaker is weighing his words with great care and uttering an extremely important and significant remark. It is a *stylistic* device and it functions to mark the word or words being articulated in this manner as standing quite apart from the surrounding utterance. It is a device frequently used by actors who are playing the rôle of interrogator. After a question has been asked two or three times, with no response from the suspect, the interrogator swings round upon him in a menacing manner and repeats the question in this very precise way, giving an impression of biting ferocity. This is the moment when the suspect yields. Jane Austen notes this bullying use of sudden articulatory precision at the end of *Emma*, when Emma has persistently refused to accept the truth of what she is being told:

> 'I am quite sure,' he replied, speaking very distinctly, 'that he told me she had accepted him.'
>
> *Emma* (422)

It should be observed that the stylistic effect depends on the fact that the sudden precision contrasts with the normal articulatory habits of the speaker. If used constantly this manner of speaking can sound wearyingly precise and pedantic, even offensively so.

The very opposite of this —'slurring' of segments, often involving *extension* of the sort we discuss in 6.9, especially of the fricatives /s/ and /ʃ/—characterizes the speech of someone who is very fatigued, or under the influence of alcohol.

It is not always possible to know quite how to interpret some descriptive words. I interpret *stiffly* as indicating the sort of precision I have been describing:

1 After sitting for a moment in silence, she said very stiffly to Elizabeth, 'I hope you are well, Miss Bennett. That lady I suppose is your mother.'

Pride and Prejudice (340)

2 'I am in favour,' said Mr Harcourt, with painful clarity of diction and a pleasing smile.

England Their England (76)

It is possible that terms like *snapped* and *rapped* might sometimes bear this interpretation.

Two examples of 'slurred' diction, indicating drunkeness, in the first case genuine, in the second feigned are:

1 'Amigoarawaysoo?' I repeated. (Am I going away soon)

David Copperfield (273)

2 'Yesh. Dining private yacht. *Eshmesheralaa.*' (Esmeralda)

Traffics and Discoveries (143)

This can be summarized as:

articulatory precision $\begin{cases} 1 \text{ normal} \qquad\quad \text{—unmarked} \\ 2 \text{ precise/slurred—expressing attitude.} \end{cases}$

6.9 Timing of segments and syllables

In speaking a speaker sets up his overall tempo and within this the listener has certain expectations about the relative lengths of different segments in different stress and intonation environments. I shall call this 'normal' length. It is however possible for a speaker to *extend* a segment or syllable, to lengthen it, for stylistic purposes, to lay special weight on a given word. Thus in *A Burnt Out Case* (36) Graham Greene writes '"We've crushed out the oil," he said with relish rolling the r.'. Here the extension has an intensificatory function.

This *extension* can also be used to modify what the speaker is saying— it turns up not infrequently in *yyyees* or *nnnooo* where the speaker signals that he is not quite sure of his opinion here. Some speakers use this device frequently to draw out the vowel of the tonic syllable, thus giving it even greater prominence. It is quite rare in life and literature and I only mention and exemplify it in passing:

1 'Cr-r-ri-key!' said Hinchcliffe, as the car on a wild cant to the left went astern.

Traffics and Discoveries (208)

2 'I never even asked who seduced her,' said Margaret, dwelling on the hated word thoughtfully.

Howards End (283)

3 'Let go, master,' he cried, almost inarticulately. 'You're ch-choking me.'

Cashel Byron's Profession (181)

Sometimes all the stressed syllables in an utterance are lengthened yielding the effect characterized as 'drawling':

A clear-cut Navy voice drawled from the clouds: 'Quiet! You gardeners there'

Traffics and Discoveries (140)

timing $\begin{cases} 1 \text{ normal} & \text{—unmarked} \\ 2 \text{ extended} & \text{—emphatic marker.} \end{cases}$

6.10 Lip setting

The posture of the lips has a profound effect upon the *sound* of the spoken message. It is quite easy to tell in listening to a radio programme if the speaker is *smiling* as he speaks, and it is often possible to hear the effect of pouting out the lips. In face to face confrontation the lip posture is, of course, startlingly more obvious and carries very important information. If the expression on the speaker's face contradicts the meaning of his words we usually take the expression on his face to indicate his *real* feeling about what he is saying. If a speaker comes in with a smile on his face and says, 'I'm very sorry to tell you I've failed that exam', the response of his listeners is likely to be 'Why are you so pleased about it?' rather than,'Oh, what a shame!'. If a speaker with no hint of a smile says, 'I'm delighted to hear about it. Nothing could make me more happy', the natural reaction is to wonder what is the matter with him, what it is that displeases him.

As with the other variables the discussion of *lip posture* will have to be simplified. For example novelists distinguish many sorts of smile: *warm smile, cold smile, generous smile, repressed smile, smile with the lips but not the eyes,* not to mention James Thurber's sinister character who when he smiled 'showed his lower teeth' *The Wonderful O* (93). Similarly there are many variations on pushing the lips forward from—*pursing his lips thoughtfully* to *she pouted delicately.* I shall however distinguish only three possibilities here—a *normal* unmarked lip posture, *smiling* and *pursed.*

People smile to express all sorts of attitudes. Here are some examples from The *Portrait of a Lady:*

1 'Well,' said Isabel, smiling, 'I'm afraid it's because she's rather vulgar that I like her'. (93)

2 Lord Warburton broke into a smile that almost denoted hope. 'Why, my dear Miss Archer,' he began to explain with the most considerable eagerness ... (132)

3 At this Ralph started, meeting the question with a strained smile. 'Do I understand you to propose that I should marry Isabel?' (181)

4 Madame Merle shook her head with a wise and now quite benignant smile. 'How very delicious! After she has done that two or three times she'll get used to it.' (209)

5 His flushed smile, for a little, seemed to sound her. 'You won't like that. You're afraid you'll see too much of me.' (292)

6 'I should have said "Wait a little longer".'
'Wait for what?'
'Well, for a little more light,' said Ralph with rather an absurd smile, while his hands found their way into his pockets. (341)

7 'Ah no, I don't forget,' said Pansy, showing her pretty teeth in a fixed smile. (386)

8 Madame Merle gave a bright, voluntary smile. 'Do you know you're a little dry?' (409)

9 Osmond took a sip of a glass of wine; he looked perfectly good-humoured. 'My dear Amy,' he answered, smiling as if he were uttering a piece of gallantry, 'I don't know anything about your convictions, but if I suspected that they interfere with mine it would be much simpler to banish *you*.' (533)

Henry James describes the expression on the faces of his characters in great detail—much more than is fashionable with modern novelists. The smiles that he mentions here have different functions. Notice however that all except 2 and 7 have one purpose in common in the extracts quoted here—they are all intended to smooth over some social difficulty which might otherwise be created by what is said. 2 is the only 'genuine' smile in the set. 4 is intended to demonstrate superior understanding. 9 is an example of a paralinguistic variable being used to suggest a different attitude from the one implied by the speaker's words. On occasions like these native speakers and foreigners alike may be at a loss. In view of these contradictions it is not clear how the message is to be interpreted. It is only in the light of long experience of the speaker and of his motives that we know that here

the verbal message represents his real intention: the smile is merely
a social gloss.

Other authors may couple smiles with more obvious attitudes—
friendliness, kindness, happiness, elation, triumph—and with more
conventional situations—greetings, congratulations, the dawning of
mutual love:

1 'Very well, thanks,' said he, grinning and avoiding her eye.
Cashel Byron's Profession (33)

2 Lydia opened her eyes fully for the first time during the conversation. 'Lucian,' she said delightedly: 'You are coming out. I
think that is the cleverest thing I ever heard you say.'
Cashel Byron's Profession (321)

3 'And whither do your meditations point?' he demanded playfully.
Tales of the Five Towns (158)

4 Celia was trying not to smile with pleasure. 'Oh, Dodo, you must
keep the cross yourself.'
Middlemarch (6)

5 'I am very glad to hear it,' said Dorothea, laughing out her words
in a bird like modulation, and looking at Will with playful
gratitude in her eyes.
Middlemarch (198)

Pursed lip posture occurs much less frequently. It is sometimes used
in addressing babies and, more rarely, pet animals. It is a lip posture
which novelists attribute to small girls when they are disappointed in
something and to young women when they are attempting to attract
young men. Perhaps no character in literature pouts so much as
David's child wife Dora in *David Copperfield:*

1 'She is a tiresome creature,' said Dora, pouting. (297)
2 Then Dora beat him, and pouted, and said, 'My poor beautiful
flowers!' (363)
3 'Oh, but we don't want any best creatures!' pouted Dora. (454)

We summarize this:

$$\text{lip setting} \begin{cases} 1 \text{ normal} & \text{—unmarked} \\ 2 \text{ smiling/pursed} & \text{—expressing attitude.} \end{cases}$$

6.11 Pause

We looked at pause in Chapter 3, where we saw how it entered into
the rhythmic structure of speech, and again in Chapter 5, where we

discussed the organization of spontaneous speech into tone groups which are typically bounded by pauses. We noted that tone groups typically contain complete syntactic structures—phrases, clauses, or sentences. It seems reasonable to suggest that whereas the advantage for the listener is that pauses function to indicate the boundaries of such structures, the advantage for the speaker is that they permit time in the stream of speech for planning the next thing to say. Sometimes a writer may indicate a pause simply to inform the reader that the character is undertaking such planning. This is what Dickens appears to be doing in this extract from David Copperfield.

> 'Why, if I was you,' said Mr Dick, considering, and looking vacantly at me, 'I should—' The contemplation of me seemed to inspire him with a sudden idea, and he added briskly, '—I should wash him!' (145)

Sometimes, however, speakers exploit pause not simply to indicate normal planning routines but for specific rhetorical purposes, in general to point up and make particularly important the part of the utterance following the pause. Indeed, one could argue that Dickens is using the pause in the above extract to do this as well, to draw attention to the simple practicality of Mr Dick's suggestion, which so well illustrates his character. It is a characteristic of 'announcer speech' on radio and television, perhaps in part intended to give the impression that what is in fact written language read aloud is actually spontaneous spoken language. In this usage the typical pattern is for a short 'comma' pause to occur before a tonic syllable:

1 It's + FIVE o'clock
2 Why don't you + LISTen in
3 Another round of + TWENty Questions

A further, rather different rhetorical use of pause occurs more generally and is found in both spontaneous conversations and in dramatic dialogue, either because a speaker is nervous or inept and finds it difficult to establish a conversational rhythm with his inter-locutor, or because the speaker deliberately manipulates the timing to put the interlocutor at a disadvantage. In such a situation, speaker A makes a comment—and utters what sounds like a syllable final tonic, falling to low, and leaves a pause. Speaker B begins to speak and at this very moment speaker A chooses to continue speaking. B is left with an uneasy feeling of having been discourteous in interrupting A and also with a feeling of frustration in that now the dialogue has moved on, the contribution he had wanted to make is no longer appropriate. The ostensible function of pause here is of course still to allow the speaker time to plan but here it conflicts with the indication of finality which the speaker has provided.

In the types of use of pause that I have discussed here, I have been concerned with the exploitation by speakers who fail to observe the normal conventions of use of the pause and, by this failure, create a particular rhetorical affect. This can be summarized as follows:

pause $\begin{cases} 1 & \text{normal pause placing} \quad\quad\quad\text{—unmarked} \\ 2 & \text{deliberately abnormal pause placing—marked.} \end{cases}$

6.12 Constructing a framework

The variables proposed here are certainly not all that need to be considered. They will however form a temporary framework for the discussion of attitude until some more satisfactory and exhaustive method of classification is developed. In their present form they can only be suggestive. I should like nonetheless to demonstrate how even this inadequate framework may be used to characterize some terms that are frequently used in literature to describe how a character is speaking. I shall present this demonstration in the form of a matrix (see pages 138–9) with the variables I have mentioned naming each row and some common descriptive terms heading each column. Where I think one variable is clearly to be preferred over another I have put a tick in the relevant row. Where an alternative seems quite likely I have put a query as well. There are a large number of ticks in the matrix and some of my assignments may certainly be challenged. This should occasion no surprise. Two actors, given the same description of an utterance that they have to render, will be likely to yield similar, but not necessarily identical, performances.

I have not attempted to discriminate very delicately between terms which describe attitude. Delicate distinctions depend not only on paralinguistic variables but also upon knowledge of the situation and of the relationship holding between the speaker and hearer. Thus there is nothing in the acoustic signal which will differentiate *confidentially* from *conspiratorially*. The appropriate descriptive term will be selected by someone who has knowledge of the situation and the characters.

I have limited this discussion of paralinguistic features to features which are directly connected with the speech process—the behaviour of the vocal cords and articulatory tract. This is, in a sense, an artificial restriction because many facial and bodily gestures contribute to the meaning of the message. Among these other features are frowning, raising of the eyebrows, widening or narrowing of the eyes or nostrils, raising or lowering of the chin, nodding or shaking of the head, shrugging of the shoulders and so on. Eventually, we must hope, a description of the function of gesture in language will appear. All I have attempted to do is consider some of the features that can be observed simply by listening to speech, without necessarily seeing the speaker.

6.13 Using the paralinguistic features

Paralinguistic vocal features are without doubt the least exploited of the resources available to those concerned with teaching listening comprehension. As we have seen, it is normally the case in spoken language that paralinguistic features reinforce the content of what is being said. Many of these features—particularly those described in terms of pitch height and range, tempo and loudness—seem to be used in very similar ways across languages; so nervousness, anger, desperation, excitement, enthusiasm, sincerity, authority, emphasis find rather similar forms of expression in terms of the features which I have been concerned to characterize. It is possible to utilize these forms of expression to guide students through taped spoken language long before they can be expected to understand all the vocabulary or the syntactic structures being used—just by becoming sensitized to these features which are often already quite familiar, but not at a conscious level, they can learn to put them to use in interpretation.

Students can begin work by identifying quite basic features—vocal indices which identify what sort of person the speaker is: whether the speaker is male or female, a child or an adult, young or old, speaking in a hurry or with plenty of time—and gradually move on to identifying who is speaking with authority and who is speaking sub- missively, who is speaking aggressively and who is speaking kindly. They can learn to identify, in, say, a broadcast discussion, who is agreeing with a previous speaker—and how do you know? Who is being polite to a previous speaker, and what are the signs of this? Who is being self-deprecating, nervous, afraid of offending and how are these states shown? Tapes of different discussions can be compared to see whether the same features are present when the same attitude is identified again.

More advanced students can be helped to use the features in a fairly precise way to follow how a speaker guides his listeners through

Paralinguistic features and attitude

	replied answered said	retorted exclaimed	important pompous responsible	depressed miserably sadly	excited	anxious worried nervous	shrill shriek scream	warmly	coldly	thoughtfully	sexily	crossly angrily	queried echoed
Pitch span													
unmarked	✓									✓			✓
extended		✓			✓	✓	✓					✓	
restricted			✓(?)	✓				✓	✓				
Placing in voice range													
unmarked	✓									✓			
raised		✓(?)			✓	✓(?)	✓(?)					✓	✓
lowered			✓(?)	✓				✓	✓		✓		
Tempo													
unmarked	✓									✓			
rapid		✓(?)			✓	✓	✓(?)					✓	✓(?)
slow			✓	✓				✓	✓		✓		
Loudness													
unmarked	✓									✓			
loud		✓	✓		✓		✓					✓	
soft				✓		✓		✓			✓		
Voice setting													
unmarked	✓									✓			
'breathy'					✓(?)		✓(?)	✓			✓		
'creaky'			✓(?)	✓					✓(?)				
Articulatory setting													
unmarked	✓									✓			
tense		✓			✓	✓	✓		✓			✓	✓
Articulatory precision													
unmarked	✓									✓			
precise		✓(?)	✓						✓			✓(?)	✓(?)
slurred				✓(?)							✓(?)		

Lip setting											
unmarked	✓	✓	✓	✓	✓	✓	✓	✓		✓	✓
smiling									✓		
pursed								(?)			✓
Direction of pitch											
unmarked	✓	✓	✓	✓	✓	✓	✓	✓	✓	✓	
rise											✓
Timing											
unmarked	✓	✓	(?)✓	✓	(?)✓	✓	✓	✓	✓	✓	✓
extended		(?)								(?)✓	
Pause											
unmarked	✓	✓	✓	✓	✓	✓	✓	✓	(?)✓	✓	✓
pause											

an argument. Here is an extract from a discussion on the British economy:

(a) //but I'm very optiMISTic
(b) //if+ + measures ARE effectively taken//
(c) + + to bring DOWN the rate of prices
(d) //then I'm VERy optimistic//
(e) //because it's a WHOLly
(f) //SPURious
(g) PROBlem//

(a)—unmarked
(b)—extended pitch span
    slow
    precise (e.g. glottal stop onset to vowel-initial *are* and *effectively*)
(c)—extended pitch span
    lowered
    slow
    'creaky'
    extended timing ([daʊːnː])

(d)—restricted pitch range
    lowered in voice range
    rapid
    slurred (e.g. *optimistic* pronounced [əptmstɪk])

(e)—lowered in voice range
    rapid

(f)—extended timing ([sːpjɔːrjəsː])

(g)—extended pitch span
    loud
    extended timing ([prɒːbləmː])

We meet the speaker as he is in the middle of expounding his view of the state of the British economy. He has been saying that he thinks Britain is in a very difficult economic situation and then goes straight into the passage I have quoted. He begins here by the straightforward statement that he is very optimistic. This is not a statement that sounds particularly convincing since it is paralinguistically quite unmarked. We may note however that the intensifier *very* is stressed, which slightly reinforces the verbal content of the remark. The listener is left, however, because of the lack of paralinguistic marking, with the impression that the speaker's enthusiasm is somewhat qualified, an impression which is immediately reinforced by the speaker proceeding immediately and without pause to *if*. The *if* is made prominent partly by the fact that it follows immediately after the preceding tone group but is itself followed by a pause, and also because it is uttered stressed, on a high pitch, thus:

opti<u>MIS</u>Tic + <u>if</u> + +<u> </u>measures <u>ARE</u> <u>effec</u>tively <u>tak</u>en

The effect of making *if* so prominent is to make the importance of the condition very powerfully marked. Still in (b), we find that each stressed syllable is pronounced slowly, which gives an effect of deliberation. This effect is further enhanced by the precision of articulation. Then the tonic word *are* is uttered with an extended pitch contour which has a strongly contrastive effect even though no overt contrast is introduced into the message. The force of this utterance seems to be:

'here I am speaking slowly and with deliberation in order to make it clear that I am making an important point. The point is that if measures are effectively taken then we have every reason to be optimistic but if effective measures are not taken then we have no reason at all to be optimistic'.

By using the high fall, the extended pitch span, on *are* the speaker implies *are not*, and what follows from *are not*, even though he does not explicitly state it. (c) begins lower than (b), the movement to the lower part of the voice range is maintained and the slow speed is maintained. On the tonic word *down* the lexical content of the word is reinforced by a pitch fall to very low, with 'creaky' voice, and long-drawn-out articulation of the vowel and nasal. The speaker is signalling that what he is saying is important, even though the utterance that he produces is somewhat deviant. Presumably he's talking about the *rate of price increases* rather than the *rate of prices*!

The next tone group, (d), echoes what the speaker said in (a). In this repetition the speaker stays in the low pitch range he has just established, but speaks rapidly and rather indistinctly, with little pitch movement on *very* and an almost inaudible articulation of *optimistic*. (d) has the effect of a filler, an utterance which simply repeats what the speaker has already said and gives him time to plan his next remark. It is made quite clear to the listener that this is indeed the function of (d) precisely by the paralinguistic features which combine to mark this as something the listener does not have to bother about. On the other hand the speaker makes it quite clear that he still holds the floor, since he continues to speak rapidly and embarks on his next remark without any perceptible pause. In (e) the rate of delivery which characterized (d) is maintained but this is slowed down by the long-drawn-out tonic words in (f) and (g). The effect of this sequence of three tonic words is very powerful. The speaker is using all the paralinguistic and intonational effects which are available to him in a normal interaction to make this point; he separates each lexical word in the phrase into a separate tone group and thus produces three tonic words: *wholly*, *spurious* and *problem*. But he links these to each other in an overall structure of the sort we observed in Chapter 5: he marks the tonic in (e) with a fall, in (f) with an extended fall, and in (g) with a loud extended fall:

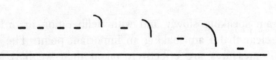

because it's a <u>WHOL</u>ly <u>SPUR</u>ious <u>PROB</u>lem

This remark is clearly signposted as the speaker's main contribution to the discussion and the listener can be in no doubt about the speaker's opinion of the significance of this particular utterance.

The function of paralinguistic features as signposts to guide the listener through the structure of an argument has only been briefly touched on here. Clearly we need more research into this area of spoken discourse. The short passage I have discussed here does exemplify the following tendency, which is characteristic of much of my data. When the speaker is making a remark which he considers to be the central point in his argument, he will make its importance clear to the listeners by marking it with some or all of the following paralinguistic features: extended pitch range, slow tempo, precise articulation, extended timing. He may speak low in his pitch range, often with 'creaky' voice, but if the remark is then to be perceived as important, he must either utter the whole remark slowly, or extend the timing of the tonic word. He may also use the intonational resources available to him of separating important words into separate tone groups, and thus making them tonic words.

7 Teaching listening comprehension

7.1 Identifying the problem

If you are trying to teach somebody something, you need to have a clear idea of what it is you are trying to teach. This is as true of teaching listening comprehension in a foreign language as it is of teaching architectural students how to draw the plans and elevations of buildings. It follows that you need to have a clear model of the desired outcome of your teaching, together with a clearly articulated strategy which specifies how you are going to bring about this desired outcome. This strategy will largely depend on your assessment of what your student already knows or can do, of the reasons why the student may not reach the point of desired outcome without some intervention from a teacher, and of what methods will be successful in helping the student to reach the desired level of expertise.

Teaching listening comprehension as a part of teaching a foreign or second language is a relatively recent development whose history lies mostly in the last thirty years. In the early days of teaching the spoken language it was assumed that students would simply acquire the ability to understand the spoken form of the language if they occasionally heard their teacher speak it or listened to a tape of it being spoken. It was quickly demonstrated that this approach was simply not working. Students whose command of English was, in other respects, admirable found it almost impossible to understand the spoken language when they eventually encountered it as it was being naturally and purposefully used in real-life contexts. It is possible to discern three major stages in the development of ideas about why competent students were encountering this problem in understanding the spoken form of the language, and hence what steps should be taken to help them cope with this problem.

7.1.1 Recognizing the code

The first stage was heavily influenced by the traditions of structuralist linguistics. It assumed that the problem for the students was that they were not able to use the phonological code sufficiently well to identify which words were being used by the speaker and how these were organized into sentences. The problem was located in the inadequate control of the phonological system because the students were relatively very much more successful at interpreting the written form of the language. Focus on the spoken forms usually began with paying particular attention to segment types which were believed to be problematic for the learners to discriminate between, which gave rise to drills in which students were required to discriminate between 'minimal pairs' of vowels like those in *bet/bat* and of consonants like those in *seize/seethe*. Then, since few languages construct their words around stressed syllables in the way that English does, there were exercises requiring the identification of the stressed syllable in polysyllabic words. Finally, at the highest level, students were required to identify whether the final pitch of an intonation contour rose or fell.

This approach, which required considerable phonetic expertise on the part of teachers if it was to be sensibly taught, was quite quickly abandoned, partly at least because it did not seem to be effective in its aim of helping students to cope with listening to the foreign language with understanding. An obvious problem with the approach from a methodological point of view was that it was preparing students to listen to words spoken slowly and clearly in isolation. They were in no way prepared to listen to spontaneous speech with its normal patterns of simplification of the sort we have discussed in Chapter 4. Similarly, the exercises on stressed syllables, stressed words, and intonation patterns were largely confined to isolated words or to short sentences spoken slowly and clearly; as we have seen in Chapters 3 and 5, such an approach necessarily ignores some of the most important functions of stress and intonation and in no way prepares students to listen to the stream of normal speech.

Perhaps as a result of disillusionment with this approach, training in coping with the phonetic signal of speech has almost completely disappeared in the 1980s as a feature of courses in listening comprehension. This seems a quite extraordinary case of throwing the baby out with the bath water. It is certainly true that the methodology which I have briefly described above is not adequate in preparing students to listen with understanding to the foreign language, partly for the reasons I have suggested—that such a methodology only prepares students to listen to words or short sentences pronounced slowly and clearly in isolation—and partly because other aspects of comprehension were ignored in such an approach (we shall discuss these in the following sections). It does not follow, however, that because the methodology was unsuccessful, the original diagnosis of the problem was at fault. There seems little doubt, as I have argued throughout, that students do indeed need help in learning to interpret the spoken form of the language and, in particular, the form of the phonetic signal. What we need to do here is to think more carefully about the appropriate methodology—a point I shall return to in 7.3.

7.1.2 Processing the complete text

A rather different approach rapidly developed which took the view that students would benefit from regular practice in listening to extended discourse. This represents a considerable advance on the previous stage where students were rarely, if at all, exposed to extended spoken discourse in the language which they were trying to learn. Now at least they had the opportunity of listening to the target language being spoken.

For many students, however, the methodology associated with this new development again posed a problem. It was quite rare that students were permitted simply to listen, and to enjoy listening, to discourse in the target language—rather they were required to demonstrate to the teacher that they had been listening and, indeed, that they had understood what they had listened to. The problem arose with how they had to demonstrate their understanding. Essentially what happened was that familiar methods which had been used for nearly a century in reading comprehension were imported into listening comprehension: students were asked to answer 'comprehension questions' on the discourse. This may not be too difficult with a written text which remains in front of you, available, as you work out the relationship of the question to the text (assuming you have understood both the text and the question). It is quite a different matter if you have listened to a spoken text which lasted, in those early days, for as much as seven minutes. What was required in order to show that you had understood a text was, at least in part, an ability to *memorise* the discourse and then to relate the questions to your memory of the discourse—this was often an extraordinarily difficult task which adult native speakers of English would frequently have had difficulty with. Students would be asked, for instance, to identify a specific word which had been uttered, to use one of the words spoken in the discourse in a new sentence in order to demonstrate its meaning, or to determine which preceding noun phrase a particular pronoun referred to. 'Understanding' seemed to imply being able to memorize the discourse (pretty well all of it), and then being able to demonstrate that you had: (i) correctly identified the words used; (ii) correctly identified the meanings of the words; and (iii) correctly identified the cohesive structure of the discourse.

Some students, particularly the academically more able ones, were good at doing 'listening comprehension' thus conceived and enjoyed these rather academic exercises. For many students, the majority, the experience was sterile and disheartening. A noticeable feature of working in a foreign language which you are not totally proficient in is that you are diminished in intelligence; in particular your memory is not as efficient as it usually is—presumably because so much of your processing capacity is taken up with actively and consciously doing in a foreign language what you would easily and unconsciously process in your own language. Less academically able students in such circumstances have considerable difficulty in remembering extended pieces of discourse, and may find it quite difficult to construct and retain an interpretation of a question and then relate that back to their fading memory of the original discourse. A reiterated humiliating experience in failing to do this adequately, merely serves to discourage the unsuccessful student from further effort. We should avoid methods which yield such discouraging outcomes and try to ensure that students enjoy experience of success in doing exercises in the foreign language.

7.1.3 Purposeful listening

Over the last ten years, as we have developed a much better understanding of the nature of the listening process, and of the processes of comprehension in general, a quite different approach to helping students with listening comprehension has been emerging. The memory problems which long pieces of discourse give rise to have been recognized; few training extracts now last longer than three minutes and many last no more than one minute. More significantly though, it has been recognized that in normal life we do not process discourse as though all of it were equally interesting or equally worthy of being remembered. In normal life we have reasons for listening, and interests and purposes which our listening serves. We are quite capable, in listening as in reading, of skimming over some bits of message which are not germane to our current purposes and then of paying particular detailed attention to those parts which seem to us most relevant. Increasingly, listening comprehension materials are being developed which reflect this—they do not require the student to process all of the discourse as though it were equally important but rather to listen for, and to select for attention, certain specific points in the discourse.

A natural development in methodology has been that, in order to meet the requirement that students should listen selectively to discourse, the discourse is presented to them in the context of a pre-specified task which puts them very much in the position of native speakers—where the point of listening is to put the information they have heard to use. In such circumstances it does not matter whether or not they have understood all the details of what was said. All that matters is that, in the context of the task, they have been able to construct enough of a reasonable interpretation to make a decent effort at completing the task successfully. They may actually have failed to pay attention to all of the discourse, they may have been unable to understand some parts of it, they may have had to infer—to work out—what the speaker must have meant. All this is practice in learning to listen as a native speaker listens. These are exactly the sorts of skills that we all use everyday in our own native language. With a reasonable view of success established, many more students now have the experience of success in listening to the foreign language.

7.1.4 The social context of listening

In the range of approaches that we have surveyed so far, the listener is viewed as a lonely individual who makes a private and individual response to what he or she hears. This is a natural assumption in a methodology largely based on traditional approaches to reading comprehension. However, once the methodology is developed to include the task-based approach described in the last section, it is obvious that it can recognize that much of our experience of listening—and indeed of interpreting—is not a lonely private experience but something which we share with other listeners. It is difficult in the classroom, if the students are to have a range of experience of listening to different native speakers of English, for the normal speaker-hearer relationship to be re-created. It is not difficult, though, to re-create the experience of listening as one of a social group, where listeners are co-operatively trying to arrive at a joint interpretation. If small groups of three or four work together to solve a problem, to complete a task, the isolated attempt to undertake an interpretation on your own which will be revealed as inadequate if you alone do not understand, can be removed.

It is clearly not going to be sufficient for most students if they are only ever asked to create joint interpretations with other students. An adult, competent user of the language must be capable of listening alone and not only understanding but also forming judgments about what was said, alone. In using this group-based approach, as with all methodologies, the teacher should use it appropriately for particular purposes at particular points in the students' development. Group working seems particularly appropriate for beginners of any age and should probably be used lavishly to begin with, but even at the beginning, it should occasionally be interspersed with pair-work and with solitary listening.

7.2 Combining the approaches

One of the unfortunate results of the more or less violent changes of paradigm in language teaching is that we constantly lose insights from earlier approaches as we turn to embrace new and more interesting ways of doing things. The rhetoric which has been developed to justify new ways of doing things often involves attacking previous practices in a wholesale condemnatory manner. I believe that we lose a great deal that is of value in resorting to this approach. I suspect that we would be wiser to adopt a more modest approach, characterized as 'standing on the shoulders of the giants of the past'. After all, past practices have usually, at the time, been extensively debated and justified in terms of the knowledge then available. In some cases, it is true, we now have better descriptions of mental processes (or at least better models), which may lead us to want to reformulate earlier views. In some other cases we may judge that the analysis of the problem was actually well founded at the time but that the methodology used in implementing this in a reading programme was unsatisfactory. In general, though, we are well advised to take seriously earlier practices and to learn from them as much as we can.

In considering some of the principles which should influence how we set about teaching listening comprehension, then, I shall frequently revert back to views which are no longer current. I shall divide the discussion of how to teach listening comprehension into two sections. The first offers an analysis of some of the problems which foreign learners (and sometimes native speakers, too) experience in understanding speech. The second section will consider some of the methods available to us to try to help our students feel more comfortable in listening. I think it is helpful to draw this clear distinction between the analysis of the problem on the one hand, and the methods available for solving it on the other. The analysis may need to be extended in the future as our understanding of the processes of comprehension grows, but the basic points in this section will retain their validity through time. Changes in methodology, however, are typically much more fundamental and are liable to be influenced by swings in fashion in language teaching to focus on different aspects of language use.

7.2.1 'Bottom up processing': the phonological code

There seems every reason to suppose that the structuralist linguists were absolutely right in identifying this level as one which it is crucial to control adequately in a foreign language (see 7.1.1). At the segmental level, students may indeed have difficulty in discriminating between some of the vowel and consonant distinctions made in English (just as some native speakers of Scottish English find it difficult to distinguish RP *pull/pool* or *cot/caught*, where the vowels are different in RP but not in Scots, or, on the other hand, some RP speakers find it difficult to distinguish Scottish English *where/wear* and *lock/loch* where the consonants are different in Scots but not in RP). The effect of not being able to identify which vowel or which consonant is being used is, obviously, that you will be unsure *which word is being used* unless there is enough contextual information to make this clear.

Since it is often the case that there is enough contextual information to allow listeners to guess which word is being used, as long as they are able to identify some parts of the word adequately, discrimination between segments is probably no more important than the ability to recognize a word even if it is much reduced in form in the stream of speech (as described in Chapter 4). The rhythmic structure of English, together with our normal tendency to do as little as is necessary to be effective—'the principle of least effort'—means that many syllables are reduced or even disappear completely in the stream of speech. The problem for foreign learners is that so much disappears in the stream of normal speech that it is not clear to them how many words there are supposed to be in the utterance and where their boundaries might lie. (This is much less of a problem for native English speakers listening to speakers of other accents of English since, despite some well-known differences of habits of simplification in different accents—for instance, whether or not you reduce /t/ in *butter* to a glottal stop—different accents do on the whole simplify in rather similar ways.)

It is essential in English to learn to pay attention to the stressed syllable of a word, since this is the best and most stable feature of the word's profile, and to those words in the stream of speech which are stressed, since these mark the richest information-bearing units. Listeners who fail to distinguish these are likely to flounder in the unstructured message (which for reasons discussed in the previous paragraph they are already having difficulty in decoding). They are likely to lose even more information if they do not know how to identify information peaks and how to use the information encoded in this distribution. On top of this, if the speaker is speaking with a set of paralinguistic features which are differently deployed from those in the listener's native language, the listener may misjudge the attitude of the speaker towards what is being said.

The foreign learner needs to learn to control the phonological code of the target language sufficiently to be able to use the richness of cues at this level— with sufficient ease to provide a constrained input for the 'top down' inference-driven interpretation to be constructed. This is, after all, the raw data of language input—without this there *is* no linguistic message, only the sort of gestural communication which infants who have not yet learnt to talk are capable of. Of course they can convey a good deal to those who know them well, which is why we should pay attention to the gestural and paralinguistic embedding of speech—but this is clearly inadequate for anyone who wants to use the foreign language to understand information encoded in it, the expression of opinion or feeling, and the expression of literary or poetic sensibility.

Learners who have progressed to the point of being able to use the phonological code competently have a good chance of being able to recognize what most of the words intended by the speaker were, how they were grouped into phrases, how they were structured into larger clauses (or sentences) and how these related to each other, together with any particularly marked attitude which the speaker revealed paralinguistically while speaking.

7.2.2 'Top down' processing: using the context to make predictions

A very striking feature of most of our adult experience of everyday language is how similar it is to language that we have heard before. Not only do people greet each other in conventional ways and talk about the weather or the lateness of the train in conventional ways but they chat, express opinions, or exchange information using for the most part a very narrow range of language, packed with large 'prefabricated' phrases like 'as far as I can see', 'to tell the truth', 'all over the place'. If we examine conversations between people we find that they constantly repeat expressions which they themselves have used as well as expressions which have been used by the other speaker.

Sometimes a speaker repeats one or more of the lexical items that the previous speaker has just used, and agrees or disagrees with this:

1   A Is it soon going to be impossible
    B No + I wouldn't say impossible + no
    A dangerous
    B ... dangerous + yere
2   Q In case I memorize them?
    A Yes + in case you memorize them
3   Q And is it true that you're still using the hospital?
    A I would say + that + erm + we are u-using + erm +
       the fringe building of the hospital + certainly

In 3 the speaker is forced into a corner by the question and appears to be playing for time with his opening gambit *I would say + that + erm*. Then he repeats a word used by the previous speaker but stuttering slightly as he says it, as though he is not quite sure that it is a correct choice, *u-using*. Then he arrives at a modification of the original question, *the fringe building of the hospital* and having thus managed to answer the question, while modifying it in a satisfactory manner, he completes the answer with a firm *certainly*.

Here are some further examples where the speaker evades a direct answer to the question but picks up and echoes part of what the previous speaker has said:

4   Q Are you optimistic about a settlement?
    A I'm an optimist + + I am hopeful that we'll leave this
       building having arrived at some kind of settlement.
    Q ... do you think this is going to satisfy your
       members?
    A well + + heh + heh + heh + + it's a question of
       arriving at a negotiated settlement + + what + eh + our
       members may accept or may have to accept + as a
       settlement + is not necessarily something that satisfies
       them.
5   Q Are you going to do something about lighting?
    A Lighting + of course + I think + is important.

In example **4**, A picks up Q's *optimistic* in *optimist* and then paraphrases it in *hopeful*. He repeats *settlement* in both answers. He picks up *satisfy* and *members* from the second question and repeats them both in his second answer. While he doesn't absolutely agree with the assumptions of the question he makes it quite clear that the vocabulary initiated by the questioner is appropriate to the situation. The more one examines records of conversations, the more one is impressed by the density of the repetition by one speaker of what the other speaker has said.

In a recent series of experiments in which 250 secondary school students were asked to participate in a series of co-operative tasks, one of the most striking features is the similarity of the language used by all of the pairs as they approached different features of each task. Each task was 'new' to them in the sense that they had not encountered just this task before but it was of a familiar kind in the sense that a task which requires one student to instruct another how to find the way from the Public Library to the railway station on an invented town plan mimics previous experience. It seems clear that adolescent native speakers (15–16 years old) use language efficiently for the most part but they use as little as is necessary to do the job in hand. They do not go in for elegant stylistic variation, typically, but keep on using the same short structures and the same vocabulary:

> you go up the High Street + and then you cross to the Gas Board + + and then turn + up the little lane there + and then you go up the next street + Head Street + left + + and then you go along to the Town Hall + and then turn left again + and then go up Church Street.

Not only does this speaker keep on using the same phrases but so do all the other 249 speakers in similar tasks. Obviously there is some variation in the phrases used and in their distribution, but the overall impression is of an astonishing similarity of language use in similar situations.

The advantage for the native speaker, in many everyday situations, is that even if you do not hear everything the other person says, you have a good idea of the sort of thing that will have been said, which you construct partly from the phonetic cues that you hear, and partly from your knowledge of what you would have said if you had been speaking, or perhaps from your stereotypic knowledge of what that sort of speaker is likely to say in such a situation. It is this familiar knowledge, which as a native speaker you have been acquiring from infancy, which allows you to cope with a very reduced phonetic input (just as it allows you to cope with a rapidly scrawled written note in a very familiar context where the content of the message is highly constrained—on the other hand, you would find it difficult to understand this same scrawled handwriting if, say, the topic was unfamiliar to you). This familiar knowledge, which has many different appellations with different shades of meaning in the literature (background knowledge, mutual knowledge, shared knowledge) derives from a range of experience which relates at least to the following features:

1 The speaker: who it is (male or female, age, level of education, RP or local accent or 'international English' accent?);
  —the role the speaker adopts in speaking (prime minister, mother, teacher, station announcer, friend);
  —the attitude of the speaker towards the listener(s) (friendly, condescending, polite, sympathetic);
  —the attitude of the speaker towards the topic (interested, bored, angry, excited).
2 The listener: who is being addressed? (Is it you?) In what role? (Pupil, child, adviser, official, a public audience—what sort?—a third party—who and in what rôle?)
3 The physical context (place and time): where is it? (Law courts, bus, radio studio, bedroom?) Different places have different sorts of language use stereotypically associated with them, as do different times (New Year, late evening, winter, etc.).
4 Genre: what sort of speaking is going on? (Public lecture, a poetry reading, an interview, a friendly chat, a news broadcast?) Different sorts of language use are associated with different genres stereotypically.
5 Topic: what is being talked about? (Race relations, literature, the price of houses, the state of the economy, a football match result, that Mrs Smith down the road has gone into hospital?)

The *topic* will largely determine the content of vocabulary items whereas the *genre* will largely determine the style of vocabulary items, so a local news broadcast might announce that 'an elderly man was knocked down by a car' (where the use of the passive obscures any attribution of guilt), whereas one neighbour might tell another 'the poor old geezer went right out and the car bashed straight into him'.

Previous experience of the way language use varies with these five features gives the native speaker an enormous advantage in bringing 'top down' processing to bear on the obscure phonetic signal, enabling him or her to narrow down expectations of what is likely to be said and, in many everyday cases, to predict very precisely what the speaker is about to say, to the extent of being able to utter the end of the sentence at the same moment as the speaker. This is most likely to happen in familiar settings. It is difficult even for native speakers where, say, the *topic* is quite unfamiliar. Thus first year undergraduates following a course on English phonetics in their own native language usually experience considerable difficulty in following the first few lectures because they do not have a sufficiently developed conceptual structure to enable them to assimilate the new information meaningfully into it—hence they are only able to do a very limited amount of 'top down' processing. Once they have begun to develop a stable conceptual structure, and they have stable representations of meaning for technical terms like 'vowel', 'phoneme', 'allophone', and 'phonetic segment', they find it much easier to follow classes. They can assimilate new information to these existing structures and so they are able to do far more efficient 'top down' processing.

The problem for foreign learners is that so much 'familiar knowledge' has to be established from scratch. They have to find out what, of their already existing familiar knowledge, can safely be imported into the knowledge base in terms of which they construct interpretations in the new language, and, depending on their aims and motivations in learning the new language, they will need to develop new sets of 'familiar knowledge' if they are to interpret the foreign language in an efficient and automatic manner.

7.2.3 Making inferences

In the last section I have been talking about using contextual knowledge to narrow down, to constrain, the interpretation of what the speaker says. It would be wrong to give the impression that the contents of this section are concerned with a wholly different kind of process, since making inferences is an activity which is particularly dependent on familiar knowledge. However, 'top down processing' focuses on the way in which familiar knowledge can be used to determine what the form of the message is likely to be or to have been in a particular context. 'Making inferences' focuses on the way in which, having decided what the message form is (or, more probably, while arriving at this), the competent listener 'knows' a good deal more than is actually specified in the message. Whether or not the native listener goes on to activate all this extra knowledge will depend on its relevance in the context of use. Let me give you an example of a very simple English sentence and the sorts of automatic processing that listeners are likely to do on it:

Do come in and sit down

1 The listener(s) are being invited into a *room* (since they are being invited to 'sit down' in it and a room is where, stereotypically, sitting is done).
2 The listener(s) addressed are not in the room.
3 The speaker is likely to be in the room (since the speaker says '*come* in').
4 The speaker is the host/hostess or the person in charge of the situation (since he or she can utter this invitation/request).
5 Listener(s) are probably being invited to sit on chairs since that is what, stereotypically, people sit on.
6 The speaker is being polite to the listener(s) (using the polite 'do-support' form, rather than simply 'come in and sit down').

Not everyone will agree with all of these inferences but most native speakers will agree with most of them and indeed will construct a mental representation of their interpretation of this sentence in which 1–6 above will be presupposed. So that if the text were to continue

The room was attractive

or

The chairs were hard

the competent reader would have no doubt about which room was referred to, or which chairs, since these would already be available in the interpretation of the first sentence. It is our ability to construct such inferences on the basis of our knowledge of the world which explains why, given a series of sentences like:

Mary was reading in the public library. Barely two yards away John was suffering from an appalling headache.

we understand that John, too, is in the public library (rather than, say, on the other side of the wall, out in the hall). We understand that John is in the library at the same time that Mary is in it (rather than a month later). Such inferences are automatic if you have the right familiar knowledge. If you do not have it, or do not understand that you must try to infer it from what is actually said in the message, you are going to have a problem of interpretation. Consider the following sentence (from *The Times Higher Education Supplement* 7 April 1989):

> The University Funding Council is to reject the Riley report recommendations for the closures of Glasgow and Cambridge veterinary schools and will ask the Ministry of Agriculture Fisheries and Food to do its sums again.

This is a good deal harder to understand unless you have the relevant background knowledge, so I will spell out in some detail first the presuppositions that are necessary, and then the inferences. First the existence of a number of entities is presupposed:

—There exists a body called the University Funding Council.
—There exists a report which recommends the closures of two veterinary schools.
—There exist veterinary schools at Glasgow and Cambridge.
—There exists a Ministry of Agriculture Fisheries and Food.
—There exist 'sums' which the Ministry has 'done'.

Now, for a full understanding of this sentence you will need to make (at least) the following inferences *over and above* identifying the words, sorting them into phrases, and parsing the sentence:

—The Riley report was a report *to* the University Funding Council (since the Council can reject its recommendations).
—The veterinary schools at Glasgow and Cambridge are part of the universities there (which is why the University Funding Council is responsible for making the decision).
—The Riley committee which wrote the report was chaired by a man called Riley (since public reports in Britain are named after their chairperson).
—The Ministry of Agriculture Fisheries and Food must have supplied some statistics to Riley's committee ('sums') on which the recommendations were based.
—The reason for the rejection of the recommendations is to do with doubt about the statistics which were presented to the committee (which is why the Ministry is to be asked to 'do its sums again').

There is little doubt that this is a hard sentence to understand—partly because it is so densely packed with information, but also because it does not make explicit the relationship between the two main clauses. It relies on the readers knowing that, since these clauses are presented together, they must be co-interpreted, and what is not explicitly stated must be inferred.

A major problem for foreign learners is developing the confidence to make constrained and relevant inferences in the interpretation of spoken (and of written) discourse.

7.3 Methodology

7.3.1 Using phonological cues

I have already suggested that foreign students are going to be particularly reliant on 'bottom up' processing in the early stages of learning the target language. This means that they need to be able to listen for the helpful cues in the language as it is used. These should always be taught in the context of meaningful use of language, and the teacher should only spend five minutes or so in each lesson on drawing attention to them, otherwise students get bored and their ability to pay attention to these details is overstretched.

When they begin to learn a new language, students are always exposed to this new language in its fullest and most explicit form. The patterns that they are required to copy and, later, to produce are either single words or short sentences carefully and slowly enunciated. In the early stages while the student is still struggling with an unfamiliar sound system, not to mention exotic syntactic and lexical forms, this is clearly the only practicable approach. Unfortunately many students progress to more complicated and sophisticated grammar and vocabulary, but do not move beyond the basic, elementary, clear and explicit pronunciation. From the point of view of their own production of the spoken language this is not a disaster—a foreigner whose command of English is not perfect is much more likely to be understood if he speaks slowly and clearly. I have already suggested that I do not approve of teaching students to *produce* 'assimilated' forms and elided forms. Sophisticated students who have been taught to be *aware* of these forms will introduce them into their own speech in a natural context when they feel able to control them. From the point of view of *understanding* ordinary spoken English the failure to move beyond the basic elementary pronunciation of spoken English must be regarded as disastrous for any student who wants to be able to cope with a native English situation. If, over a number of years, he has consistently been exposed to a form of spoken English in which the segments are explicitly articulated and the contrast between stressed and unstressed syllables thereby partially obscured, the student will have learnt to rely on acoustic signals which will be denied him when he encounters the normal English of native speakers. It is therefore essential that, as soon as the student begins to be capable of understanding quite small pieces of structured English, he should be exposed to some English as it is normally spoken. Otherwise he will learn to rely on un-English signals and he will have no reason to learn English signals.

When this suggestion is made, teachers often complain that their students will not understand this sort of spoken English. Of course they will not. They need to be taught how to understand it, and, just as any other area of teaching a foreign language is presented in graded stages, so must the comprehension of the spoken language be. To begin with only two or three short sentences, with very familiar structures and vocabulary should be presented. If the student does not understand what is being said the first time the sequence must be repeated until he does understand it. Ideally the material should be presented on a record or tape. Then the identical signal can be played again and again. It is very hard for a teacher, who sees that a class does not understand what he is saying at first, to avoid putting in extra information when he repeats the utterance. It is also very difficult, even for a native speaker, to stand in front of a class which he is used to addressing in slow, deliberate pronunciation and suddenly to produce normal English speech. A further advantage of using taped or recorded material is that the session can be clearly labelled a 'listening' session. If the students are used to the idea of their teacher's pronunciation being a model for their own, this avoids the difficulty of their using his informal speech as a model at too early a stage in the foreign language learning process. As the students progress they should be able to cope with the teacher speaking English in a more and more normal fashion.

Just what material is used for 'listening' exercises will of course vary with the age and sophistication of the students. The main thing is to avoid anything that was originally produced specifically for foreign use. It is extremely difficult for speakers who know that they are producing material for foreign listeners not to speak more clearly than they normally would. Teachers who are able to receive BBC broadcasts are obviously in a strong position. Programmes for pre-school native English speakers contain simple stories and nursery rhymes and, often, instructions for simple physical exercises. The stories and rhymes are very repetitive—they tend to be spoken with big pauses between each tone group so that the child has plenty of op-portunity to process the content of the tone group—but within each tone group the correct rhythm of stress and unstress is preserved and a certain amount of normal phonetic simplification goes on. This sort of material can very well be used for primary school English teaching. For older students some of the schools programmes for primary and secondary English schools contain suitable material and adult students can be exposed to news items—just one short and simple one to begin with. The advantage of news items is that the adult's own general knowledge will equip him with much of the background information so that he can make intelligent guesses about what must be being said long before he can be supposed to 'know' all the structures that are being used or all the vocabulary. Regular listening to news broadcasts builds up familiarity with well specified areas of vocabulary—the vocabulary of air disasters, of party politics, of weather forecasting.

For those who have no access to BBC broadcasts, recordings of various kinds made for native English speakers provide valuable material for 'listening' sessions. There are many recordings of favourite folk and fairy stories. For older students there are recordings of plays. The advantages of recordings is of course that they can be played over and over again until the students have understood them.

Well-equipped establishments with audio-visual aids at their disposal can use films made for English classrooms of scientific experiments and geographical features. Here the commentary is spoken by a native English speaker who is making no special concessions to foreigners but is speaking reasonably clearly and slowly. Even in this speech there will be many examples of phonetic simplification however. Again, the advantage with films is that the students can see them many times over if necessary.

There are now many listening comprehension courses on the market. The best of these present a wide variety of English speech spoken by different individuals in natural situations. They include interviews and conversations between individuals who are quite unaware that their utterances will have to be understood by foreign students. Having acquired some reasonable listening material, what is the teacher to do with it? For young children it is probably not possible to do much at first other than simply expose them regularly to normal spoken English. For older students it is important to develop different *techniques* of listening and to encourage them to become *aware* of what signals they rely on in listening to their mother tongue, what signals they rely on in listening to slow colloquial

English and what signals they must use in listening to normal informal English.

Let us consider first the signals which we employ in interpreting the message. We listen for paralinguistic signals and we watch for gestural signals like frowns, puckered brows, narrowed eyes in order to advise us about how the speaker feels about what has been said. This should guide us to make certain predictions about how he will reply. In listening to spoken English we listen and we watch for indications of stress placement—the nodding of the head, twitching of any part of the anatomy, louder and longer syllables—in order to identify the meaningful words in the utterance. We listen for pauses to mark the edges of tone groups, 'sense' groups, and we listen and watch for the tonic syllable—an extra large muscular movement, and extra long syllable with a pitch movement on it—and this identifies the focus of information in the tone group. We try to identify the lexical items by grouping the unstressed syllables round the stressed syllables and making some sort of prediction about the syntactic structure that we have here—which items have got to be nouns and which must be verbs—are the nouns preceded by articles and/or adjectives. Meanwhile we consider the vowel qualities in the stressed syllables and what the movement of the edges of these vowels tells us about the consonants in the vicinity—whereabouts in the mouth are the consonants formed, what happens to the voicing at the end of the vowel, is it cut off sharply before a 'voiceless' consonant or does it tail away into a whisper in a 'voiced' consonant. If the speaker is in front of us we look for the facial signals of the segments—for the lips approaching each other, the amount of movement of the jaw, the protrusion or rounding of the lips. And we consider the total length of the utterance in relation to what has gone before—we consider the syntactic structuring of what the speaker has already said—the lexical items that have been used already in this context. What sensible hypothesis can we construct about what the speaker is saying or has just finished saying?

Some of these signals will be very like those the student uses in his own language—especially many of the paralinguistic features and the markers which show the division of the utterance into 'sense groups'. Speakers of many languages need to be helped to use the stress signal that is so important in English. Students need to be taught to recognize the sound of a stressed syllable in an utterance. Broadcasts, tapes and records can all be used in constructing exercises in which students are required to identify stressed syllables and/or meaningful words. If this is a difficult exercise the teacher must be prepared to spend a lot of time helping students to recognize the different variables which mark stress—greater pitch prominence, greater duration, greater amplitude, greater precision of vowel and consonant articulation. Where films are available a very useful exercise is to switch off the sound track and have the students signal whenever the speaker utters a stressed syllable. With most native speakers this is very clearly marked by extra muscular effort of the jaw and lips or by muscular movements of the head, eyebrows, shoulders and so on. Similar exercises can be devised to help students learn to recognize the tonic syllable.

For students who find difficulty in recognizing some sets of English consonants, tapes and records provide valuable listening exercises. Study, for instance, the recognition of final 'voiceless' stops in normal passages of speech. Teach the students to become aware of the shortness of the preceding vowel and the cutting off of the vowel by a glottal stop. Teach them to listen to final 'voiced' fricatives and to recognize the length of the preceding vowel and the shortness of the fricative. Where films are available turn off the sound track and study during a few sentences all examples of the realization of /r/—what, if any, facial signals of this consonant are there? Study English /f/ and /v/ where these are pronounced differently from the mother tongue and notice the diminished facial signal in English. Where the students experience specific segmental difficulties—both in perception and production—expose them to the difficult segments, as much as possible. Have them listen to a sentence or two containing the difficult segments again and again and try to make them aware not only what the segment is like in its 'central' 'ideal' form, but what effect does it have on surrounding segments and what effect do they have on it.

English vowels provide a notoriously difficult hurdle in pronunciation teaching. Fortunately in comprehension teaching this difficulty is much less important. The student who is exposed to a sentence in context does not have to worry too much about 'what vowel' he hears. He has to recognize a *word* and a word that is possible in that context. It is very rare in real life to be in doubt whether *the sheriff was shot through the heart* or whether *he was shot through the hat*, whether *John bit the dog* or *John beat the dog*. Clearly an ability to distinguish these vowels will help in the selection of the suitable word but the context will usually make this selection reasonably straightforward.

In drawing attention to phonetic detail you may find it useful to concentrate sometimes on a series of similar events—for example, half a dozen final voiceless stops—and sometimes, particularly with more advanced students, to work systematically through a short utterance asking questions like:

—Is there one word here which is particularly clear?
—What is that word?
—Are there other words which are relatively easy to hear? What are they?
—Write down what you can hear leaving gaps for the bits you cannot hear properly. Can you guess what must be going to fill those gaps? Are there any stressed syllables/consonants/vowels which suggest that you are right?

It is important to recognize that there are very rarely absolutely 'correct' answers to such questions, so they should not be treated as if there were. Many judgements about clarity or prominence will be, to some extent at any rate, relative. Rather such an exercise should be used to draw students' attention to helpful cues which are present in the phonetic signal.

In paying attention to these phonetic details, it is important to discuss their function, particularly with advanced students. If the speaker pronounces one word particularly loudly and clearly, is this because the word is being used to introduce 'new' or 'contrastive' information into the discourse? Is it because the speaker is reaching the climax of what he is saying at this point? If a syllable appears to be considerably lengthened, is this to indicate a stressed syllable—and if so, why is that particular word being stressed?—or is it to indicate the last word in a phrase before a pause, that is, a grammatical boundary? Or both?

7.3.2 Learning to use contextual information

In 7.2.2 we saw the major features of context which a competent listener will make more or less use of, appropriately, on different occasions. Obvious exercises of a very general nature to sensitize students to the effect of these features would be rôle play. Characterize a particular type of speaker, say, as a rather stern grandmother with a passion for tidiness, and speculate about how she would address a grandchild who spills paint on the carpet, or as a tightfisted bank manager approached by an indigent would-be borrower, or as a benign customs officer trying to explain to a harassed traveller why you cannot bring fresh meat across national boundaries. Such exercises are quite open-ended and should, I think, be seen as an opportunity to help the students to construct a range of stereotypes appropriate to the target language.

A much more constrained type of exercise can be developed with more structured topics where again students need to begin by considering who is speaking to whom and on what occasion and what sorts of remarks, in this context, such a speaker might be expected to make. The class can develop a list of facts/opinions which could be written on the board as they come up with them, then, when what relevant familiar knowledge they have is activated, they can listen to a short tape of what the speaker actually said, and see whose predictions were nearest to being correct. This is a particularly helpful type of exercise since the teacher can smuggle into the preliminary discussion a range of relevant vocabulary items, some of which will turn up in the discourse which the class is about to listen to—you should be careful though, to keep this as an incidental bonus and not let the class degenerate into 'spot the word' listening.

An even more constrained type of exercise can be developed where students do not make predictions about context based simply on the social and external features of context but are also allowed to listen to a minute or two of the discourse before the class discussion begins. Now, the previous discourse can itself be used as part of the constraining context. Here students might be asked to provide the next sentence, to complete a sentence which the teacher has cut off in the middle (where the syntax of what has already been uttered will serve as a further constraining feature), or they might be asked to propose the next word or phrase. Once again a range of alternatives proposed by different students can be written on the board, and advanced students should offer a brief justification of each proposal. (It is important in 'part of a sentence' exercises that the teacher choose a reasonably clearly articulated part of the tape so that there is likely to be agreement on what it is that follows. At least you should be careful to do this to begin with. More advanced students could be asked to handle the situation where it is not entirely clear what it is that the speaker has said.)

Many of us must have had the experience of having mentally finished a sentence for a speaker long before the speaker himself has finished uttering it. The sentence we have mentally completed may differ in small details from what the speaker actually finishes up with, but it is essentially the same in the overall meaning of the message. It is particularly easy to do this with someone we know very well personally, or someone whose public expressions of opinion we are well acquainted with. And it is particularly easy to do this when whatever the speaker is going to add is largely predictable from what we already know of the subject under discussion, of what has been said so far, and of the textual structure that the speaker is speaking in. For example if a speaker who speaks in coherent, well formed sentences begins *On the one hand we may prefer to go into Europe*—a reasonable prediction for the end of this sentence might be *and on the other (hand) (we might prefer) to stay out.* The details of the message—whether the speaker repeats *hand* and *we might prefer* or not, and whether he chooses some other lexical item rather than *stay*—such as *remain* or *keep*—may be not exactly the same as the predicted version but the essential meaning of the message is the same. The ability to make intelligent guesses about what the speaker must be going to say is clearly shown by the fact that it is possible for speaker A to complete a sentence and for speaker B to begin to answer it immediately. Speaker B must have predicted the end of A's sentence and at least begun to structure his reply by the time he begins to speak. The same sort of process can be observed in the reading aloud of young children when they are just learning to read fluently. Very often they will not read aloud exactly what is written on the page but some perfectly intelligent substitute—for example they will miss out or insert *and*s and *but*s in a perfectly reasonable manner. They will replace proper names by pronouns or vice versa. They will replace one past tense form by another—*have come* by *came.* The message that they read aloud is usually a perfectly acceptable re-interpretation of the original message. Anyone listening to the child reading aloud without carefully reading the text at the same time would not guess that there was any deviation from the text. It is this ability to make an intelligent guess about what the message must be which enables the child to understand rapidly without having to read each separate letter, and the listener to understand rapidly without having to listen to each successive sound.

Clearly training in making intelligent guesses will play an important part in learning to understand the spoken form of a foreign language. Early exercises might take the form of carefully controlled 'sentence completion' exercises. The sentences must first be thoroughly contextualized and well controlled for grammatical structure—as in the *on the one hand—on the other* example. The part of the sentence that is the stimulus can then be played and the students asked to make a reasonable guess about how it would end. To begin with the teacher would require the students to add only one or two words, but later more words can be required. This is a demanding exercise for the teacher in that there is no single 'correct' answer. He must be prepared to approve any response which the student can justify in terms of the factors we have already mentioned—general knowledge of the subject, what has been said already, the syntactic structure of the first part of the sentence.

It is not always possible to predict how a speaker will finish his sentence. Sometimes indeed a speaker can say something which we do not understand at all. We think about it for a moment and then ask the speaker to repeat what he said. Very often, even before he begins the repetition, the sentence that he must have said dawns suddenly upon us, not partially understood but totally understood. It is as though in the time since the speaker began the utterance, the subconscious mind of the listener has been scanning and rescanning the acoustic signal trying to assign a possible interpretation to it—then suddenly, though in more time than an interpretation usually takes, the meaning of the sentence is understood. There are several points we can make about this sort of processing technique. It is obviously not different in *kind* from that which predicts the end of the sentence before the speaker has finished—the listener still relies on his ability to make an intelligent guess. It is obvious that the listener can store the whole signal in his short term memory while he scans it to try to interpret it. Often, as I have suggested, he understands the whole structure of the message, all the words and their relation to each other, suddenly, apparently all at once. Sometimes however he works out what the structure of the sentence must have been and asks a specific question about the filler of some slot in the structure—

What was it you said John hid?
Who did you say hid the papers?
What did John do to the papers?

It would be interesting to know how much information the listener needs to be able to work on before he stops trying to work out the answer and simply asks the question *What did you say?*. If, for example, he hears only

---------------papers

would he be able to ask a question

Who did *what* with the papers?

My impression is that such questions are rare and that listeners usually only query one item in the structure. We should note that even among native speakers who know each other quite well it is occasionally made clear that one native speaker has formed an incorrect hypothesis about something that another native speaker has said. I shall tell you a personal anecdote to illustrate this. A colleague of mine was talking about playing croquet when he was young and he remarked that on one occasion in a competition he had won 'a fire guard'. A moment later a third person came into the room and I repeated what we had just been saying. At this point my colleague said 'it wasn't a fire guard but a flower vase'. Now you may like to consider what clues I must have used to arrive at my interpretation—two stressed syllables with the tonic one first—a compound word—correct vowel values (fire guard—['fɑ'gɑd], flower vase—['flɑ'vɑz])—two CVC syllables in each case the first one beginning with /f/—some piece of domestic equipment small enough to be presented as a prize. The only reason why I ever knew that my hypothesis was wrong was that I almost immediately repeated what I had understood in the hearing of the person who had spoken the original message and he was able to correct it. It would be interesting to know how many times a day we all arrive at a hypothesis about something which has been said to us which is, strictly, an incorrect hypothesis, but which is never revealed to us as incorrect because the opportunity for correction does not arise. The fact of the native speaker's behaviour, is that he makes his hypothesis and carries on as though that were the correct hypothesis. In some unknown, but presumably large, percentage of cases he is correct and is shown to be so simply by the fact that most of his assumptions are not contradicted as he carries on his everyday life. We have to teach the foreign learner to behave with the same confidence—to make a reasonable interpretation even though he has not clearly heard all the information.

So far I have talked about using taped material and developing contexts within which such discourse can be interpreted. It should not be forgotten, though, that the most obvious and frequent context within which the students will experience the spoken form of the target language will be in the classroom itself. It cannot be overemphasized that the teacher should use spoken English as often as possible and for as many purposes as possible in the classroom. Some teachers are embarrassed about their own command of English and fear that they may be offering their students inadequate models. An occasional lapse in your own English is much less important than failing to offer your students the opportunity of hearing English actually being used purposefully in the context of their own lives. Very few teachers of English who are not native speakers have perfect English (and indeed not all native speakers control standard English perfectly). All of us are, in varying degrees, inadequate models. The crucial point for our students is that they are actually offered models, even though the models are imperfect. They will learn English much faster in a classroom where some sort of English is used as much as possible in a meaningful way, so that they have lots of contextual cues to understanding, and begin to build up stereotypes of familiar expressions, than one in which the teacher simply greets them in the target language and then lapses into the mother tongue. This is the very basis on which learning to interpret the target language using context is built. Ideally it will be supplemented by frequent use of a range of tapes which will gradually introduce the students to a range of native speakers of English beginning with the appropriate target model—RP, American, or Australian—and then moving on to other major accents of English.

7.3.3 Drawing constrained inferences

I have treated 'top down' processing as though it were largely concerned in creating initial expectations of what an utterance will contain, and 'inferencing' as though this were what the listener does having heard the utterance, to make sense of it in context. From a theoretical point of view this almost certainly misrepresents the way we process, since it seems likely that all of these processes are going on simultaneously, in parallel. However, I think it is helpful from a pedagogical point of view to consider that there are three points of view from which you can focus on the interpretation of an utterance:

1 Before the utterance, while you activate relevant familiar knowledge, and 'predict' what the speaker is likely to say in more or less specific terms.
2 During the utterance, while you pay attention to the phonetic/phonological detail and observe how these offer cues to the speaker's structuring of the utterance.
3 After the utterance, as you try to work out, to infer, what the speaker meant by uttering that remark at that point in the discourse.

Research into how we draw inferences, enough and no more than those necessary for the interpretation of the discourse for our current purposes, is, in my opinion, the most interesting current problem in pragmatics. We are clearly capable of adjusting the level of inferencing from a very sketchy outline for some mundane, everyday utterance to a large, elaborative structure in the interpretation of a work of literature. In general we will try to infer co-operatively what we think the speaker intends, but sometimes we infer over and above that, elaboratively, and infer, for instance, that the speaker is not actually convinced by what he himself is saying at this point. We can infer then, not only from the linguistic signal but also from the context of utterance, which will include the way the speaker utters the message. How can we help our students to draw appropriate inferences so that they can construct adequate interpretations?

I fear that we are not yet in a position to approach this problem in an orderly way. We can, however, to begin with, make it clear to students that inferencing is a necessary part of interpretation and that they should not expect to find everything explicitly spelt out in the text itself (otherwise every text would have to be interminably long and repetitive) and we can draw attention to some of the general principles which appear to pervade efficient human processing.

Consider the two sentences:

The king died.
Then the queen died of grief.

It is possible to process these as two individual events in time. At some time, in some place, the king dies. At another (later) time, in another place, a quite unconnected queen dies. It is my impression that in the early stages of interpreting a foreign language that is as far as some students would get in understanding this text. Simply coping with the foreign language takes up so much of their processing capacity that they do not perform normal inferencing on the discourse. However, most competent listeners will assume a closer relationship than this between the facts described in these sentences. They will infer that there is a narrative at issue here. They will infer that 'the queen' was the wife of 'the king', and that she died soon after he died. Over and above that, competent interpreters will probably infer elaboratively, thereby creating the beginnings of a romance, that the queen died of grief *because* the king had died. This is not a necessary inference but it is a very reasonable one. You might find it interesting to explore how many of your students actually succeed in drawing such inferences.

There is a generalization to be made about drawing inferences: process as *parsimoniously* as possible. If two events are mentioned, assume that they are related. If two times seem to be at issue, check to see if they can be simultaneous, if not, try to make them as closely sequential as possible. If two places seem to be at issue, check to see if they can be different ways of referring to the same place, or if one is part of the other, otherwise assume that they are as close to each other as possible. If two individuals seem to be at issue, check to see if they might be one person (for instance with a series of expressions like *Barnaby* and *Barney,* or *Barnaby* and *he*). In general, create as constrained an interpretation as possible.

The important point for students and teachers to grasp is that it is frequently the case that a lot of the content that we understand from a discourse is not actually stated at all. Inferences which we make unconsciously and automatically as competent readers or listeners in our own langauge, we may quite fail to make in the foreign language because we feel that somehow we should only interpret the language that is actually used, and that if we worked at it, somehow the text itself would yield some more explicit information. It can be positively beneficial to work out with students how a particular interpretation is achieved, showing them the step-by-step low level processes which we normally take for granted, and showing them how a great deal of the content that we understand from a discourse may not actually be stated at all. Compare the two 'texts' below:

(a) He accumulated debts. He married an heiress.
(b) He married an heiress. He accumulated debts.

In both we infer that the first-mentioned event happened first (as we always do unless specifically told otherwise). In spite of the fact that the two texts both contain exactly the same sentences, we now interpret them quite differently. We assume that 'he' in (a) first accumulated debts and then married an heiress, and moreover that he married her cynically, in order to pay off his debts. In (b) we make no particular assumption about his reason for marrying, which was, we assume, the mark of the beginning of an extravagant lifestyle which led to him accumulating debts. This extra information is not contained in the forms of the language—it is information which the competent interpreter must infer, from reading the second sentence in each 'text' in the context of the first, and in the light of stereotypical expectations of what happens to people who marry heiresses.

It would be a mistake to spend a great deal of time in every class in paying detailed attention to the processes of interpretation, but it is certainly worth while for the teacher to check from time to time that students are creating an appropriate level of inferencing in their interpretation and, with a difficult text it may be worth while spending some time on working out with the class, step-by-step, how an interpretation is achieved. (This can usefully be done in pairs or groups and then compared.) It is important to choose an interesting text for such an exercise, one where the students can enjoy the identification of inferences. This can be a particularly illuminating mode of studying tapes of dramatic interaction (and indeed it is often a necessary mode in the study of poetry).

7.4 Conclusion: the active listener

It is easy, in trying to teach 'receptive skills', to allow students to drift into a passive role. I believe that this leads rapidly to boredom on the part of the students and often, failure to learn much from the class. It is essential to encourage active participation by the listener—to listen predictively and critically, watching out for new information which fits neatly into already existing conceptual structures and reacting sharply, and indeed often accusingly, when confronted with information which does not fit into the preconceived framework. This is a normal sort of reaction from many of us in everyday life: we cannot afford to have too many changes in our conceptual structures— we just find ourselves overburdened, bewildered and lost. We tend to prefer to hear confirmation of our own cherished opinions and beliefs. This naturally conservative tendency can be usefully exploited in comprehension classes (both listening and reading). From time to time the students can be challenged to cope with some information which does not fit neatly into their established scheme of things. This can be a hard exercise in a foreign language but it is important that intermediate and advanced students begin to experience language which does not simply restate what they already know or could have guessed but which is insufficiently structured to yield a clear message, or yields a message which is not directly compatible with what they already know.

It is possible to construct many types of exercise for small groups of students to undertake co-operatively which will exploit such characteristic features of language use. I shall describe just two types. You could make a tape (2–3 minutes long in all) where four suspects in a murder/theft/arson case describe their movements just before the crime. Two of the accounts would fit together quite well, but the third speaker is nervous and muddled, and the last one is trying to deceive. The students are invited to listen to the tape and to determine who is lying; they have to cope here with a set of accounts of the world which are not self-consistent and coherent, and they have to listen critically to spot the inconsistencies. This again is the sort of task which lends itself to group work, where one member of the group is allocated the rôle of 'scribe' and is asked to write down in four columns what was happening at any given time. The other members of the group are responsible for telling the scribe what each of the characters is doing. The task here is simply to look for the guilty party and to justify this identification.

The second type of task is one which is deliberately constructed to give the students practice in coping with insufficiently specified verbal messages—a phenomenon which is all too common in life, but much less common in many listening comprehension courses. A tape can be constructed which gives instructions about how to do some task, say in what order to feed animals in a zoo. The students would listen to the tape, in small groups once again, and follow the instructions while relating them to a plan of the zoo which they have in front of them and which is marked with cages and enclosures for different animals. Some of the instructions should be ambiguous: 'the big cats need their meat at 3 p.m.' might leave in doubt whether the pumas or the jaguars are being referred to, or both. Some instructions might appear initially to be contradictory in that, having been told 'the bears must be fed at noon', there is a later instruction which says 'the bears need their fish at 1.30 p.m.'. However, the active listener will note that there are both brown bears and polar bears in the zoo plan, and will infer that it is the polar bears which will eat fish (this inference being based on familiar knowledge) *or* will be encouraged to *check* which bears should be fed at which time. As ordinary human beings in everyday life, we constantly encounter partial, underspecified, information. The active listener recognizes this, and, when it matters, follows it up and checks it out. The uncertainty in a foreign language will obviously be greater since the code input will itself be much less efficiently processed. We need to help the student become better able to process the phonological cues—this is what this book is mainly about—and to be better able to use contextual information appropriately and to infer appropriately and thus build reasonable interpretations. Perhaps the most important contribution we can make is to help our students listen to the foreign language with such a feeling of confidence that they are able to ask questions, just like a competent native listener, when they have failed to understand something. The good listener is not someone who understands correctly all of the time; by such a stringent criterion all of us would fail. The good listener is someone who constructs reasonable interpretations on the basis of an underspecified input and recognizes when more specific information is required. The active listener asks for the needed information. Our goal is producing good active listeners.

Appendix

Rules for pronouncing orthographic *h* and *ng*
Most people will be familiar with these rules, but I state them here
for those who are not familiar with the relationship between orthography and pronunciation.

(a) *h* is pronounced initially in all words except *heir, hour, honest*
and *honour* and their derivatives (*heirloom, hourglass, dishonour*
etc.).

h is pronounced medially except in a few words following the
prefix *ex-: exhaust, exhibit, exhilarate* and their derivatives.

(b) *ng* is pronounced as [ŋg]
  (i) medially in a word when it is not immediately followed by
      a suffix. E.g. *finger, linger, mingle, singular, anger, language.*
  (ii) when it occurs at the end of a stem which is immediately
       followed by the comparative or superlative suffixes *-er* and
       -est: longer, longest, stronger, strongest.

  Elsewhere *ng* is pronounced [ŋ]. E.g.
  (i) word finally: *sing, long, thing, tongue.*
  (ii) medially before suffixes other than the comparative *-er* and
       superlative *-est: singer, singing, hanger, hanging, longing.*

Works quoted from in Chapter 6

Jane Austen *Mansfield Park*. Everyman's Library no. 1023. 1963.

Jane Austen *Pride and Prejudice*. World Classics. 1962.

Jane Austen *Emma*. World Classics. 1963.

Arnold Bennett *Tales of the Five Towns*. Chatto and Windus. 1910.

Charlotte Brontë *Jane Eyre*. Smith, Elder and Company. 1906.

Joseph Conrad *Amy Foster* and *Typhoon* in *The Nigger of the Narcissus and Other Stories*. Penguin Books. 1963.

Charles Dickens *David Copperfield*. The Caxton Publishing Company, London.

George Eliot *Middlemarch*. Everyman's Library no. 854. 1930.

F. Scott Fitzgerald *Tender is the Night*. Penguin Books. 1967.

Ford Maddox Ford *The Good Soldier*. Vintage Books. 1951.

E. M. Forster *Howards End*. Penguin Books. 1963.

Graham Greene *A Burnt Out Case*. Penguin Books. 1961.

Thomas Hardy *Return of the Native*. Macmillan. 1926.

Thomas Hardy *Tess of the D'Urbevilles*. Macmillan. 1922.

Henry James *Portrait of a Lady*. Penguin Books. 1949.

Rudyard Kipling *Traffics and Discoveries*. Macmillan. 1904.

A. G. MacDonell *England Their England*. 1962.

A. A. Milne *The House at Pooh Corner*. Methuen. 1937.

Bernard Shaw *Cashel Byron's Profession*. Constable. 1924.

Bernard Shaw *You Never Can Tell* in *The Complete Plays of Bernard Shaw*. Adams Press Ltd.

C. P. Snow *Time of Hope*. Penguin Books. 1949.

Muriel Spark *The Girls of Slender Means*. Penguin Books. 1966.

R. L. Stevenson *The Wrong Box*. Longman. 1889.

James Thurber *The 13 Clocks* and *The Wonderful O*. Puffin Books. 1967.

P. G. Wodehouse *The Inimitable Jeeves*. Penguin Books. 1958.

Bibliography

Abercrombie, D. (1964a) *English Phonetic Texts*, Faber and Faber.

Abercrombie, D. (1964b) 'Syllable quantity and enclitics in English' in D. Abercrombie, D. B. Fry, P. A. D. McCarthy, N. C. Scott, and J. L. M. Trim (eds) *In Honour of Daniel Jones*, Longman.

Abercrombie, D. (1967) *Elements of General Phonetics*, Edinburgh University Press.

Albrow, K. H. (1968) *The Rhythm and Intonation of Spoken English*, Longman.

Boomer, D. S. and Laver, J. D. M. (1968) 'Slips of the tongue' in *British Journal of Disorders of Communication* 3, 2–12.

Brazil, D., Coulthard, M. and Johns, C. (1980) *Discourse Intonation and Language Teaching*, Longman.

Brown, G. and Yule, G. (1983) *Teaching the Spoken Language*, Cambridge University Press.

Chomsky, N. and Halle, M. (1968) *The Sound Pattern of English*, Harper and Row.

Crystal, D, and Davy, D. (1975) *Advanced Conversational English*, Longman.

Crystal, D. (1969) *Prosodic Systems and Intonation in English*, Cambridge University Press.

Crystal, D. (1976) *The English Tone of Voice*, Edward Arnold.

Dictionary of Contemporary English (1978) Longman.

English Pronouncing Dictionary (1978) Dent.

Gimson, A. C. (1962 and 1970) *An Introduction to the Pronunciation of English*, Edward Arnold.

Halliday, M. A. K. (1968) *Intonation and Grammar in British English*, Mouton.

Halliday, M. A. K. (1970 *A Course in Spoken English*, Oxford University Press.

Jones, D. (1918) *The Pronunciation of English*, Cambridge University Press.

Jones, D. (1962) *An Outline of English Phonetics*, W. Heffer & Sons.

Laver, J. D. (1980) *The Phonetic Description of Voice Quality*, Cambridge University Press.

Leech, G. (1974) *Semantics*, Penguin Books.

Lyons, J. (1972) 'Human Language' in Hinde, R. A. (ed.) *Non-verbal Communication*, Cambridge University Press.

O'Connor, J. D. and Arnold, G. F. (1961 and 1973) *Intonation of Colloquial English*, Longman.

Palmer, L. R. (1936) *Introduction to Modern Linguistics*, Macmillan.

Quirk, R., Greenbaum, S., Leech, G. and Svartvik, J. (1973) *A Grammar of Contemporary English*, Longman.
Roach, P. (1983) *English Phonetics and Phonology*, Cambridge University Press.
Ward, Ida C. (1945) *The Phonetics of English*, W. Heffer & Sons.
Wells, J. C. (1982) *Accents of English 2: The British Isles*, Cambridge University Press.

Index